Terminal Destruction

Nicholas Norman Adams

Terminal Destruction

Capitalism, Technology, Accelerationism and The Decline Within Immediate Modernity

palgrave
macmillan

Nicholas Norman Adams
The School of Health
Robert Gordon University
Aberdeen, UK

ISBN 978-3-032-22273-2 ISBN 978-3-032-22274-9 (eBook)
https://doi.org/10.1007/978-3-032-22274-9

This Palgrave Macmillan imprint is published by the registered company Springer Nature Switzerland AG
The registered company address is: Gewerbestrasse 11, 6330 Cham, Switzerland

Acknowledgements

This book is dedicated to those no longer here: Anne Lilian Smith, Neil Ross, Debra Gimlin, Katie Ralfs.

It would be impossible not to acknowledge some authors, theorists, and artists whose works have influenced my own writings: John Healy, William S. Burroughs, William S. Burroughs Jr., Hubert Selby Jr., Ryū Murakami, William Gibson, Harlan Ellison; Mark Fisher, Erving Goffman, Nick Land, Ccru, Sadie Plant; Roberta Williams, Veda Hlubinka-Cook, Joachim Trier, Masamune Shirow.

Prologue

There are no tomorrows; tomorrows can't be relied on to come in this vagrant society. Nothing can be taken for granted. Each day you have to prove yourself anew in toughness or lack of it.

John Healy (1988, *The Grass Arena*)

It was a difficult decision to begin researching and writing this work. My unease was linked to several factors. Firstly, we as people: the social actors that make up the fabrics of society, ill-require another literary reminder of how bleak the present climate of reality can be. As I write this in mid-2025 there are numerous reasons to feel depressed about the structural and cultural decline in the UK and globally. However, to recognise and track the status of cultural decline and the causal factors that shape this present—or *immediate*—state, I felt that a work that brought together some progressed, diverse perspectives that build upon existing thinking would overall represent a valuable contribution to social theory: spotlighting a pathway forward for reigniting interest in what I loosely term *decline studies*. So, I forged forward with the writing regardless of the negative possibilities the developing work telegraphed. Secondly, I considered when working with the core theorising underpinning the connective contributions in this work, how people may *feel* reading the material. This is partly due to my background as a research psychologist (with some prior clinical experience), and in equal part due to my own lens vis-à-vis sensemaking of life and its ups and downs. In all honesty, some

of this writing surely makes for a depressing read; but, hopefully within 'the darkness' there are glimmers of illumination that can trigger new directions in thought and approach: this is my only goal with this work and I maintain the standpoint that 'the darkness' can cause these fragments of light to shine more intensely. Thus 'darkness' is not a negative construct: it is a component of balance. Thirdly and lastly, this work focusses on interrogating the present *decline* of *immediate modernity* and visualises structures underpinning this *decline*—giving new language and theory for which to discuss and examine influencing factors, but: I offer no real solutions (beyond speculative approaches) as to how the present *decline* trajectory may be paused, realigned or reversed. Instead, I offer only a series of conceptualisations and structural frameworks from which such *decline* may be better understood so that others can unify in discussions to develop solutions. While this is the initial step, it's up to you to remix, combine, execute, re-circuit and reinterpret the content of this publication in any useful ways that you see fit.
Good luck.

June 2025 Nicholas Norman Adams

Contents

About the Author

Nicholas Norman Adams is an interdisciplinary Psychologist and Sociologist. He received his PhD from the University of Aberdeen in 2019. His primary research interests are identity, risk-taking, accelerationism, technology, and anxiety, and how these constructs intersect in ways that can be used to understand the present culture of Western society. He is employed as a permanent Research Fellow at Robert Gordon University. He lives in Leith, Scotland.

CHAPTER 1

Introduction: Capitalism, Technology, Accelerationism, and *The Decline*

Soon, even your brain will be metal!
The 'Metals Fetishist' from Tetsuo: The Iron Man (1989, directed, written, produced and edited by Shinya Tsukamoto)

Abstract This introductory chapter establishes the conceptual frame of *immediate modernity*, outlining the key ideas and terminology that structure the following chapters. It introduces *The Decline* as a lens through which to understand contemporary culture's acceleration towards collapse under the intertwined forces of technology and capital. Rather than offering fixed conclusions, this collective work presents a flexible theoretical toolkit for interpreting a rapidly changing world, positioning acceleration, deterritorialisation, and technocapital as defining dynamics of the present moment. In doing so, it prepares the groundwork for the analyses developed in the following chapters.

Keyword Immediate modernity · The Decline · Technocapitalism · Accelerationism

This work sets out to explore our present technological reality via the lens of *immediate modernity*: a culture increasingly accelerating towards a terminal destruction. I term this process *The Decline*.

N. N. Adams, *Terminal Destruction*,
https://doi.org/10.1007/978-3-032-22274-9_1

The overarching goal of the work is to link together and expand various useful theoretical touchstones and relevancies, applying these as a means of demonstrating the absurdity of the present moment: its unsustainability and self-destructiveness. Primarily this work interconnects the present *decline* state of society with heavy acceleration (i.e. constant, rapid increases) in technology, technological reliance by humans on machines, and the means by which technology and capitalism have become interlinked as a techno-hegemony in frames that construct negative psychological 'fallout', and then present the anxious effects of technological reliance as a natural, inescapable and (paradoxically) beneficial product of modern society to human actors.

Through a process of spotlighting and connecting, this work provides an overlay: *a toolkit* to reframe and reconceptualise these hegemonic social processes, instigating a changed lens from which to understand the immediate reality human actors currently exist within and how this represents a culture locked into a trajectory of terminal destruction and what this trajectory looks like.

In the spirit of getting straight to the point: I've always found lengthy introductions, while a significant trend within academic writing, largely superfluous to social theory work. Borrowing a sentiment from Taleb's work *Antifragile*: there is often little functional requirement to understand all aspects of a specific concept, construct or idea; instead, the most practical function and useful approach is often localised towards understanding only *how* a specific idea can be conceptualised and applied in ways that one can make this notion meaningfully applicable in a given context or situation (Taleb, 2012) and how this operationalisation may be useful to one's own understanding and to that of others. In short, there is no one-size-fits-all with regard to how to apply social theory and whether it can be defined as relevant or not: relevance is dependent on numerous diverse mechanisms and nuances of application, and the temporality and context within which theory is applied. Indeed, the idea of providing a long, in-depth introduction to this work is further rendered obsolete by the rapidly accelerating nature of society (more on this later: see Chapters 2 and 3), for almost as soon as a contemporary theory has been conjured to explain, interrogate or give meaning to a phenomenon, society evolves to render this theory in immediate need of reactive updating and augmentation. To this end, I find it pointless to introduce with a delineation of what this work contains and how it can be used beyond what I have already said, for as soon as an application is argued as relevant, the foundation of this relevance is near-immediately delocalised—deterritorialised—as a proof-of-concept for which to validate the theory. A helpful analogy here is to consider modern theory-building to occur not on a solid concrete foundation, but on a bed of constantly shifting sand. Thus, rather than present this work as a collection of structurally sound and readily assembled theories that stand the test of time, I rather present this as a movable tent which can be pitched anywhere and rapidly uprooted to be relocalised within a constantly shifting landscape. As such, through dynamism and adaptability, I hope to avoid the dilemma of developing something which is immediately obsolete due to the structures upon which it has been developed reconfiguring.

To briefly summarise, if you're a social theorist, social scientist, and/or anyone else with an interest in challenging the present structures of society linking with increasing technologicalisation, capitalisation, and the commodification of humans, and you're noticing an undeniable decline across all components of social process: disconnection, disinterest, anhedonia, that people are busy-but-bored, and general unhappiness and lack of meaning are abundant, then keep reading, you might get something out of this. If not, don't worry; if you bought this from a sympathetic bookstore, they might refund you; if not, and you can stand to take the hit on the cover price, leave it somewhere interesting, and perhaps someone else might read it and take something from it.

Thank you for the opportunity.

Reference

Taleb, N. N. (2012). *Antifragile: How to live in a world we don't understand.* Allen Lane.

CHAPTER 2

Defining Immediate Modernity

Modernity is a qualitative, not a chronological, category.
Theodor Adorno (1951, Minima Moralia: Reflections from Damaged Life)

Abstract This chapter defines *immediate modernity* as a temporal condition in which anticipation and reflection have been overwritten by an enforced, algorithmic present. Time no longer flows but accumulates: layered, compressed, and rendered flat through digital intensities. Drawing on Land, Fisher, Suarez-Villa, Rosa, and others, it argues that technological development has become inseparable from capitalist logic, embedding accumulation within 'innovation' itself. Acceleration paradoxically operates as both mechanism of stability and driver of collapse; this creates a contradictory culture of forced progress, sustained by anxiety, and perpetually on the edge of implosion.

Keywords Immediate modernity · Technocapitalism · Social acceleration · Temporal compression · Hauntology

In the 1995 Manga movie *Kôkaku kidôtai—aka Ghost in the Shell*, written by Shirow Masamune and Kazunori Itô, and directed by Mamoru Oshii, the central character Major Motoko Kusanagi states:

N. N. Adams, *Terminal Destruction*,
https://doi.org/10.1007/978-3-032-22274-9_2

> If we all reacted the same way, we'd be predictable, and there's always more than one way to view a situation. What's true for the group is also true for the individual. It's simple: Overspecialise, and you breed in weakness. It's slow death.

Kusanagi is here referring to differences between cybernetically and technologically augmented and 'enhanced' bodies and minds, and that of the slightly and non-enhanced 'natural' bodies and minds. In this scene, Kusanagi, who is herself a heavily augmented cyborg whose only 'original' human components are a portion of her biological brain and her spinal cord, is engaged in a discussion with her colleague, Togusa: a man with little cybernetic enhancements aside from an implanted communications chip in his brain. Togusa is questioning Kusanagi about the value to both himself—internally—and to Kusanagi—externally—that he can possibly bring to her special operations unit, given his body is less augmented than those of Kusanagi and her colleagues, and thus, less physically strong, resilient, and 'capable'. Kusanagi replies by highlighting that the strength of Togusa's contribution lies in his diversity from the existing members of her team—Section 9—disowning the benefits of a collective overreliance on technology to achieve operational goals, and discarding the perspective that cybernetic augmentations equate to a naturally superior or inherently more capable human operator. Kusanagi points out that individuals with different lived experience, naturally divergent perceptions and bodily, cognitive, and perceptive differences are necessary in a unified cultural context where actors are brought together to collaborate; to achieve a strategic common goal. The importance Kusanagi places on this collaboration is to avoid homogeneity at all costs, equating this homogenised uniform 'sameness' as inevitably resulting in a "slow death" due to such uniformity breeding-in inherent weaknesses as a product of engineered conformity and overreliance on a duplication of like-actors with the same skills and similar ways of thinking. This conformity is propagated under the misattribution that homogeneity makes collaboration easier and society more cohesive, as all actors are operating against the same background structures. But the opposite is true.

While drawn from science fiction, the above scene contains a powerful metaphor, and draws similarities to the present situation facing social actors in *immediate modernity*: the issue of hegemonic conformity and uniformity being mistakenly framed as a strength that leads to a smoother and more socially cohesive functioning of society. In actuality, this breeds in weakness as a 'naturalised' product of striving for regularity. This is the essence of capitalism and capitalist structuring in *immediate modernity*—the achievement of an embedded hegemonic cultural acceptance: a belief that social actors in Western society must subscribe to a commerce-based capital existence to fulfil manufactured desires, wants and needs. Capitalism offers only two sanctioned destinations: success and wellbeing. Yet the route towards either is fundamentally deceptive. Hegemony 'works' through a familiar carrot-and-stick logic in which people keep moving but never advance. The subject ages in place, expending energy on a motion that resembles progress while delivering none. What is promised always drifts just beyond reach, and most people die long before the horizon ever comes into view. This is the slow death of conformity that Major Kusanagi identifies. It is not a dramatic collapse but a gradual wearing down that functions as a core feature of *immediate modernity*. Life becomes a cycle of anxious striving without arrival, a paradox state of static momentum within which movement replaces progress and the idealised attainment remains perpetually unattainable.

Several works have established the above paradigm using different language, theory, and examples, and situated the mechanisms of this hegemony within late modernity with finesse. This book interprets these works at different times and in different ways as components of wider theorising. Two of Mark Fisher's works: *Capitalist realism: Is there no alternative?* (Fisher, 2022a) and Fisher's posthumous compilation: *Postcapitalist desire: The final lectures* (Fisher, 2020) are important here. Interpreting Fisher's works: these masterfully deconstruct capitalist hegemony as capitalist realism, with Fisher using the term as a vehicle to describe a kind of *cultural common sense*: the deeply embedded assumption that capitalism is not only the 'natural' dominant structural system for making sense of society, but is positioned as the only system that could realistically exist as a governing blueprint for a society so complex. Capitalist realism functions less like a clearly defined ideology and more like a background atmosphere, quietly shaping what can be imagined, hoped for, or acted upon. Instead of attempting to wholly graph the structures of capitalist realism, Fisher explores how this condition functions via a lens of subterfuge control (an argument similarly rooted in Gramsci's notions of hegemony which I will invoke via a different framing later), and how this ascendancy shapes how we feel, think, and relate to time. Fisher's notion of *the slow cancellation of the future*—borrowed from Franco 'Bifo' Berardi's *After the Future* (Berardi, 2011)—captures something deeply familiar: the sense that our capacity to imagine real, systemic change is steadily drifting away; being readily eroded as society continues to accelerate forward, but towards a future that is unknown and feels stagnant, just like the context of the present. The present no longer feels like a springboard for possibility but increasingly more like a holding pattern, where novelty takes on a substance: a *feeling* that social actors are experiencing a *remix of the past*: a reality where alternative futures feel progressively out of reach. As such, to be moving forward is now to also be moving backwards, experiencing a form of anxious nostalgia as culture, art, music, and so-called important cultural touchstones are recycled as rehashes of past trends. Thus, the present and future are both *hauntological*. Neoliberalism's reach into all areas of life: education, culture, relationships, even inner life, has made it harder and harder to imagine anything outside of its capital-structural logics. So: instead of fuelling hopeful trajectories, technology and culture reinforce a kind of paradoxical immediate 'stuckness': a circuit-looping of old forms, a saturation of the present, and a steady decline in the belief that things could be otherwise. It should be noted here that Fisher's argument isn't totally fatalistic. His work is an invitation to notice this condition, to name it, and resist against it by reclaiming the possibility of different futures, however uncertain their possibility may seem.

Now that this foundational stance has been outlined, the best forward position from which to unpack a heightened understanding of the 'trap' of the networked capitalist structuring of society is via constructing language to describe *immediate modernity* in detail. For this position an examination of the link between technology and capitalism can be extrapolated, and how the primary inescapable effect of this dominant relationship across society is felt by human actors as anxiety. However, prior to this I find it prudent to first include a section providing clarity over how some of the notions described above, and indeed the foundational concepts from which such ideas have evolved, are utilised within this work as theory.

Important context on use of Psychoanalysis, Fisher, and the methodological frame of *Immediate Modernity*

Undoubtedly Fisher's work occupies a distinctive position within the psychoanalytic–materialist tradition, drawing force from the uneasy confluence of Lacan's psychic topology and a Marxian critique of production, mediation, and desire. Fisher's account of capitalist realism is most interconnected to this inheritance (Fisher, 2022a). Further, behind the polemical clarity of Fisher's writings lies a Freudo-Lacanian architecture in which the Real, the Symbolic, and the Imaginary[1] (Lacan, 1988) interact to sustain the ideological *reality principle* of late capitalism. The psychic economy that Fisher diagnoses and discusses in capitalist realism—the pervasive conviction that *there is no alternative*—operates as a collective defence mechanism: a repression of the Real of social antagonism displaced into the Imaginary of consumption and the Symbolic order of work, debt, and mediated enjoyment. Capitalist realism, in this sense, represents a cultural mood, a social symptom, and a pathology of desire that reproduces itself across both individual and institutional registers. Lacan's tripartite schema is particularly instructive for understanding Fisher's manoeuvres. The Real marks the traumatic kernel of social contradiction; the Symbolic gives this contradiction linguistic and ideological form; and the Imaginary supplies the perceived coherence that allows (or inflicts) the subject to bear it. Fisher's enduring interest in these dynamics is evident also in his discussions of depression and impasse: affective states that signal much less motifs of personal weakness (although the self-imposed feelings of inadequacy brought upon actors via social framing features heavily, see Fisher, 2014a, 2014b) but also the psychic registration of structural contradictions (Fisher, 2022a). Here Fisher echoes the Marx-Freud syntheses of the twentieth century: Fromm, Reich, Marcuse, in which libido and labour are mutually determining—parallel—processes. Fisher's reactivation of these lines through contemporary media culture produces what could be framed as a psychosocial realism: a style of analysis that reads the psyche as an infrastructure of capital, and capital as an infrastructure of the psyche.

To foreground this lineage is also to explicate the methodological frame that guides *immediate modernity*. To clarify, I do not approach Fisher's works as a doctrinal authority but as a generative interlocutor: a point of departure for rereading the present through a composite lens that draws equally from Deleuze & Guattari's desiring-machines,[2] Nick Land's

[1] To define clarity re psychoanalytic term usages from the outset, where I refer to Lacanian concepts of the Real, the Symbolic, and the Imaginary in this book, these notions are capitalised, when referring differently to the material-world as *the real*, and various symbolism and imaginary concepts, there are not capitalised, to illustrate distinction.

[2] Deleuze & Guattari (1972) overturn the idea that desire arises from lack, which in psychoanalytic terms is the sense of an inner absence waiting to be filled. Lack is not inherent but manufactured: a disciplinary narrative that keeps subjects tethered to promises that cannot be met. In its place, they frame desire as an active and generative force. Their 'desiring-machines' describe how desire moves through linked flows that

'libidinal materialism' notions,[3] and various complementary and juxtaposed currents within psychodynamic psychology, interpretive mediations on technology, and thinking vis-à-vis the rapid social shifts in the present temporality. This orientation resonates with Michel Foucault's oft-cited characterisation of his own work as a 'tool-box': a set of conceptual instruments to be taken up, reassembled, and applied to the contingencies of a given problem rather than preserved as doctrine. The theory of *immediate modernity* adopts a similar ethos, treating Fisher and Land's ideas not as closed systems but as a reservoir of analytic tools to be refunctioned across differing theoretical and disciplinary terrains—oscillated, framed, and refocussed through varying additional lenses. In this sense, I maintain that theoretical fidelity is much less important than conceptual utility: the capacity of an idea to illuminate contemporary configurations of subjectivity, power, and mediation.

Speaking to the above, Fisher's psychoanalytic inheritance, while salient, is recontextualised in this work within a broader interpretive ecology of forces that extends into the circuitry of the digital, the economic, and the technocultural: i.e. the co-evolutionary nexus of

generate relations and effects across the *body without organs*, which is not a literal body but a conceptual field where intensities circulate before being organised into stable forms. It is the surface on which connections are made and unmade, the site of potentiality prior to social coding. I argue in this work that these dynamics always operate within wider infrastructures that regulate and redirect desire, and in *immediate modernity* this regulation becomes constant and totalising, with capitalism functioning as the dominant machine that captures, channels and limits what desire can attach to. Human experience, in this frame, becomes a circulation of productive connections shaped by a system invested in sustaining the fiction of lack while extracting value from the intensities that desire continually produces.

[3] Nick Land's libidinal materialism treats desire as a material force that precedes and exceeds the human. It is not psychological or symbolic but an energetic pressure in the world itself, cutting through subjects, systems and histories. Land pushes Deleuze & Guattari's desiring-production to its outer limit, recasting it as an inhuman thermodynamic field where desire operates as a current of acceleration, depletion and intensification. Capitalism becomes the machinic infrastructure most attuned to these forces—the system that amplifies and circulates libidinal flows with the least resistance. Within this ontology, the human is little more than a transient formation, briefly cohering in a torrent of energies that far surpass conscious intention. Read through *immediate modernity*, libidinal materialism exposes a world driven by escalating impulses and structural overheat, where subjectivity strains to hold its shape inside a reality organised around ever-faster extraction, excitation and dissolution.

technology and culture, wherein machines, networks, and mediatic environments inscribe and are reciprocally inscribed by the Symbolic orders, subjectivities, and lived practices of a given social moment. The arguments in this work largely unfold from this stance: that to grasp the psychic conditions of *immediate modernity* we must read varying components of psychoanalysis *with* and *against* its own humanist residues, tracing how its insights on desire and repression mutate within an automated, algorithmic landscape.

This orientation, particularly when focussed to interrogate anxiety in the present cultural moment (as in Chapter 3) finds an unexpected (and at least theoretical) ally in the work of the British social psychologist and therapist David Smail, whose work also requires acknowledgement. Smail's *materialist psychiatry* spotlights a counterpoint to both the privatisation of distress and the abstracted idealism of much theoretical psychoanalysis (Smail, 2018a, 2018b, 2018c). Smail argues (like Fisher) that suffering is not an internal malfunction but a social relation: power, class, and economic insecurity leave indelible psychic marks. Smail's concept of 'outward' causation similarly networks with Fisher's claim that depression is the rational affect of a culture without agency (Fisher, 2014b). By situating Smail's conceptual notions in proximity with Fisher, I aim to emphasise how material power and psychic life are co-produced, and how any project of critique must move between the Symbolic infrastructures of ideology and the material infrastructures of social control. Where Fisher reads the depressive subject as the symptom of capitalist realism, Smail provides the therapeutic inversion: the means to return that symptom to its social origin. At the same time, my synthesis in this work diverges from both Fisher's and Smail's frames in important ways. Whereas Fisher remained anchored in the Lacanian topography of lack and often the melancholic repetition of the lost object, *immediate modernity* experiments with more fluid, Deleuzo-Guattarian conceptions of desire as production and of the subject as a dividual node within broader machinic assemblages. Desire here is not absence, but process; repression is replaced by modulation. This theoretical migration from 'the clinic' to 'the circuit' re-situates the psyche within the technological and economic accelerations of the twenty-first century, what I call *The Decline* state.

Similarly, I provide some early clarity and acknowledgement here of Suarez-Villa's work on *Technocapitalism* (2001, 2003, 2012, 2013). Suárez-Villa's account of technocapitalism represents an instructive backdrop for understanding the conditions from which *immediate modernity* emerges and evolves. Suarez-Villa's arguments that contemporary capitalism is defined not simply by the commodification of goods but by the systematic exploitation of creativity, innovation, and technological knowledge resonate strongly with the *immediate modernity* frame. Unpacking this: the productive core of technocapitalism lies in the extraction and enclosure of human imagination: the maintenance of Gramscian *hegemony*—the subsumption of invention itself into circuits of accumulation, repetition, and replication. This process marks a profound shift in how both labour and subjectivity are organised: the inventive capacities of individuals and collectives become raw material for capital's expansion. Through this lens, the *technocultural* becomes the lived expression of technocapitalism's logic: the sphere in which culture, psyche, and technology converge as sites of value production and psychic capture. The self is reconfigured as a technocultural interface: both a producer of digital artefacts and a product of algorithmic feedback. In this sense, *immediate modernity* extends Suárez-Villa's diagnosis into the experiential and affective dimensions of technocapitalism, examining how these logics manifest not only economically but phenomenologically. The result is a model of subjectivity perpetually in negotiation with systems of technological mediation, within which the boundaries between production, communication, and cognition have effectively and paradoxically merged/collapsed.

These interpretive shifts employed throughout this work are, by design, provocative. The aim is not to correct Fisher (nor any others cited) but to reroute conceptualisations through alternate genealogies, exposing how various psychoanalytic grammars can be retooled for a world in which consciousness is increasingly networked, externalised, and automated. Under this light, *immediate modernity* as a concept proceeds as both homage and departure: an effort to sustain Fisher's concern with the psychic life of capital while extending it through a more experimental synthesis that draws psychoanalysis into contact with sociotechnical systems, additional cybernetic theory, and applied psychological thought. The Lacanian registers remain present, but they are here rethreaded (and relocated) through a plural set of interpretive contemporary machines whose frictions, I argue, produce new analytic traction on the crises of subjectivity that define the present *immediate modernity*.

The below section represents conceptual coordinates, clarifying terms for the preceding sections of this work and how they are utilised. The terms defined here are not intended as fixed categories but as working coordinates: conceptual anchors that orient the reader through a theoretical terrain that is, by its nature, mobile and contested. Each term functions less as a fixed definition than as a living device: provisional, adaptive, and responsive to the contexts in which it is used.

Immediate modernity names the historical–psychological condition that this book seeks to theorise. It describes the present as a state of unmediated saturation, where technological, economic, and affective processes converge in real-time and collapse the buffers through which experience was once processed. The 'immediacy' here refers not to transparency or directness but to a condition of continual exposure—an overproximity of the subject to information, affect, and acceleration. *Immediate modernity* is thus both temporal and phenomenological: a modernity stripped of its modernist distance, in which the future no longer unfolds but arrives all at once. It marks the culmination of what Fisher termed *the slow cancellation of the future*, though extended here into an account of how the self navigates this density of the now.

Accelerationism, throughout this book, is approached as a contested conceptual lineage rather than a doctrine. The notation /Acc is used throughout as shorthand for the accelerationist family of thought: a cluster of positions exploring the relationship between capitalist dynamics and technological and/or social speed. Right accelerationism (R/Acc) valorises market forces and the productive chaos of capital; left accelerationism (L/Acc) seeks to appropriate technological modernity for emancipatory ends; and unconditional accelerationism (U/Acc) views acceleration itself as an autonomous process that exceeds political containment. My concern is less with adjudicating between these strands than with tracing how they imagine the relationship between agency and velocity as a concept of progression. Accelerationism here names an interpretive vector: the recognition that social, economic, and psychic processes have entered a positive-feedback loop in which speed[4] becomes both symptom and structure.

Social Acceleration (as theorised by Hartmut Rosa, see 2010, 2013) operates in a different but related register. Where accelerationism offers

[4] Although speed is one element of accelerationism, I do not reduce the concept to velocity alone. Across this book and developed in detail within Chapters 5 and 6, I treat accelerationism as a broader structural dynamic: an intensification of feedback, abstraction, and recursive mediation within *immediate modernity*, where systems amplify and reinforce their own operations beyond simple questions of pace.

a philosophical or political engagement with the dynamics of modernity, Rosa's framework is sociological and diagnostic, emphasising the temporal compression of everyday life: the speeding up of technological innovation, social change, and the rhythms of individual experience. Rosa's analysis captures how temporal intensification generates alienation and desynchronisation. The distinction between Rosa's social acceleration and accelerationism proper is therefore one of emphasis: the former examines the empirical texture of time under late modernity, while the latter engages its metaphysical and political implications. In *immediate modernity* these frameworks intersect—Rosa's temporal sociology grounds the affective experience of acceleration, while the accelerationist debates reveal its philosophical stakes.

Deterritorialisation and **Reterritorialisation**: these concepts are drawn from Deleuze & Guattari's *Anti-Oedipus* (1972) and *A Thousand Plateaus* (1982). Deterritorialisation describes the process by which stable social, symbolic, or psychic configurations are dissolved—flows of capital, desire, or meaning escape the boundaries that once contained them. Reterritorialisation, conversely, marks the reimposition of order, the moment when those flows are captured anew within fresh codes or structures. Together, these terms map the oscillatory logic of contemporary existence: every liberation of desire or technology is quickly folded back into new regimes of control. Within *immediate modernity*, deterritorialisation and reterritorialisation are not sequential stages but simultaneous operations: the constant unbinding and re-binding of the social and the subjective.

Fragmentation/The Subject: This fluidity extends to the status of the subject itself, captured through the distinction between the individual and the dividual, and the process of dividuation. Interpreting Deleuze's later writings (Deleuze, 1992; Deleuze & Guattari, 1982), the dividual (in *immediate modernity*) designates a subject no longer whole or self-identical but distributed across digital networks, data profiles, and algorithmic traces. Under *immediate modernity*, subjectivity becomes both fragmented and externalised: the person exists as a composite of informational residues that circulate beyond conscious control. Dividuation thus describes a new ontological condition of selfhood under techno-capitalism, where identity is processed rather than possessed. This figure of the dividual displaces the autonomous individual of liberal humanism, aligning with Fisher's insights into the dissolution of psychic coherence under neoliberalism but extending them into the domain of computational mediation. This is referred to in this work as a fragmentation of 'the self' through digital engagements.

The uncanny, as Fisher mobilises the term, underpins the affective texture of this entire landscape. Ostensibly derived from Freud's *Das Unheimliche* (Freud, 2018), the uncanny (as interpreted for *immediate modernity*) spotlights the moment when the familiar becomes strange, when repression returns as a 'ghostly' aesthetic or emotional disturbance. For Fisher, the uncanny serves as a reading of the cultural logics of late capitalism: the spectral persistence of lost futures, the eerie recurrence of forms detached from historical continuity. Within *immediate modernity*, the uncanny interconnects as an atmosphere and a diagnostic: the motif indexes the subject's disorientation amid recursive technologies and exhausted imaginaries, but absent *real* novelty. It signals that our temporal and affective infrastructures have become haunted by their own obsolescence and replications: an existential feedback effect of a system that cannot innovate yet cannot stop accelerating, reproducing, and amplifying, but in manners constrained by the restrictive hegemony within which these actions occur.

Taken together, the above concepts provide vocabulary for navigating the theoretical and affective terrain of *immediate modernity*. They articulate a world in which technological speed, psychic fragmentation, and cultural exhaustion intertwine; where deterritorialisation no longer promises liberation but perpetual circulation; where subjectivity itself has become dividuated, and where the uncanny replaces the new dominant affect of experience.

2.1 The 'Real' Start Point of this Work

Within the contemporary reality of *immediate modernity* it has become undeniable that human anxiety has increased to a near ever-present 'ghost emotion'[5] for many social actors (Giffort, 2022). While 'anxiety' framings have shifted across modernity, from the 1960s anxiety concepts have centralised on individualist clinical, and linked psychological, neurological, and biochemical theories of human anxiety (Horwitz,

[5] I use this term to refer to the all-pervasive and ever-present yet highly normalised experience of anxiety as a 'baseline' emotional response to the structures of *immediate modernity*.

2013; Kenwood et al., 2022). Reactive to this thinking, some cultural scholars have approached examination of societal shifts and lifestyle occurrences that may provide explanations for rapid macro-level societal anxiety increases that interconnect on a more socially encompassing level than stand-alone psychological-biological theories (Crombez, 2018, 2021; Nigmatullina, & Rodossky, 2022; Rafter, 2001; Rosa, 2010, 2013; Shri, 2010; Suarez-Villa, 2012, 2013). However, social theorising of anxiety as a product of modernity is overall limited. Critical to progress investigations further is to acknowledge that much existing psychological scholarship still defines anxiety per narrow individualistic clinical sense-making, often eschewing interrogation of changes to the complex macro-behavioural and social components of wider human society that can reveal markers of collective 'anxious change'. Such markers often link with accepted micro-focussed clinical definitions, such as: "a feeling of unease [...] worry or fear, [...] mild or severe" (NHS, 2022). As opposed to conceptualising these negative shifts on an individual, psychological level, in reality such unease and dissonant discomforts often occur collectively, and may be examined more readily (and indeed, more authentically) by interrogating broader social trends, namely human and technology interactions and narratives (Crombez, 2021; Rosa, 2010, 2013, Rosa et al., 2017; Suarez-Villa, 2012). This valuable, realist perspective represents less a challenge to established neurobiological anxiety theories, but rather a complement to conceptualising and tracking human anxiety through micro-level metrics and measurement scales. While such scales are typically constructed at a macro level, these are routinely applied at a micro-individualistic level to define, measure, and diagnose 'anxiety' prevalence, severity, and social trend, and legitimise anxiety as an individual disorder (Bagby et al., 2004; Beck et al., 1993; Fullana & Shackman, 2023; Lee & Stein, 2023; Tanaka & Chen, 2023). This dichotomic stance, alongside valuable progress already made by the above scholars, begs the question:

> If anxiety in immediate modernity occurs primarily as a collective social experience, why does society continue to treat anxiety as an individual psychological problem?

The above quandary should not be presented as entirely novel thinking. Mark Fisher's work on capitalist realism and the spectre of technological shifts that permeate late modernity does a masterful job of deconstructing linkages between specific media, politics and technologies, and interrogating how social transmutations are felt on a human, collective societal level in the West (Fisher, 2014a, 2017, 2018, 2022b). Fisher's theorising also examines notions of mental anguish, and trends for conceptualising anxious experiences in late modernity (Fisher, 2014a, 2022b). At the core of Fisher's work on understanding a contemporary anxious pandemic, Fisher suggests that social trends for framing negative mental experience as individual, privately experienced 'damage' precludes any true understandings of the scale and impacts of depression-anxiety and the related ability to understand depression as a negative collective experience (Fisher, 2017, 2022b).

Some scholarships have made forward progress aligning with Fisher's perspectives. Notably, Crombez (2018, 2021) explores the exponentially increasing logical structuring of modern society as constructing manifold anxious notions in human actors, akin to Fisher (2017, 2022b), emphasising the psychological dichotomy of framing collectively-experienced anxiety as a product of individualistic biomedical disruptions alone. Reactive to this position, Crombez spotlights a sociological-biopsychosocial approach, networking a critical method into linkages between ongoing evolutions in modern and postmodern societies, new forms of technology-mediated existence and associated social and identity (re)configurations. As an output, Crombez proposes a new method for the diagnosis and treatment of anxiety: critical socioanalysis (Crombez, 2018, 2021).

Like Crombez, Suarez-Villa (2012, 2013) develops interconnections between modern capitalist accelerations as a paradoxical output of late-capitalist technological and scientific advances. Suarez-Villa links these accelerations to an overarching *logicalisation* of social existence, where creativity and personal expression are commodified, bending to conform to the structuring architecture of a hyperised capitalist apex (Suarez-Villa, 2012). While Crombez reacts to this by providing a framework of socioanalysis as an output of theorising, Suarez-Villa introduces the post-industrial descriptor *Technocapitalism*, arguing that macro-level technological advances are so interconnected with capitalist structures as to near-universally de facto programme new technologies, advances, and relational threads of power to propagate and replicate key capitalist structuring principles as a proxy of their proposed intentions. As such, the *circuits* of capital replicate their own structures of progress. This is a theme explored in depth previously and extensively by Nick Land (1993, 2009, 2012, 2017).

A clarifying note is important here to differentiate technocapital and its sub-domains: throughout this work on *immediate modernity*, the term technocapital is reinterpreted/utilised to describe the convergence of technological systems and capitalist value production: the *machinic* synthesis through which capital extends its reach into every register of social and psychic life. Technocapital is not a monolithic domain but a multiplex field composed of heterogeneous sub-systems, each with its own temporalities, degrees of automation, and modes of capture. It is more accurate to speak of *pervasive technocapital* as an overarching condition: the infrastructural logic that binds together networks of computation, finance, logistics, and affective mediation, while recognising specific technocapital sub-domains that operate per distinct principles. For example, platformic labour deterritorialises work by externalising productive activity into algorithmically managed ecosystems of self-branding, data extraction, and precarity. High-frequency trading, by contrast, exemplifies deterritorialisation at the micro-temporal level: capital itself operates through machinic speeds that exclude human cognition, generating a regime of automated abstraction. Meanwhile, pharmaceutical and biotech markets deterritorialise at the somatic and molecular scale, fusing capital accumulation with biopolitical control and the pharmacological modulation of affect. These domains share a common grammar of extraction and automation yet differ in their vector of deterritorialisation—that is, in the level at which they dissolve and reconstitute the social or the bodily. Each represents a distinct articulation of technocapital's wider logic: the continuous conversion of human, biological, and informational capacities into profit through technical mediation. Recognising this multiplicity enables a more precise reading of how deterritorialisation functions across the contemporary landscape. It prevents the conceptual inflation of technocapital into a singular, unanalysable totality and instead situates it as a differentiated ecology of machinic processes. Accordingly, when *immediate modernity* refers to technocapital, it designates both this pervasive infrastructural logic and its heterogeneous instantiations. The theoretical emphasis falls on how these sub-domains intersect to form an *immediate* social field—one in which financial, algorithmic, pharmacological, and affective circuits operate concurrently and recursively. This distinction sharpens the analytic scope of this book: technocapital is not an 'area for application' but the composite condition through which contemporary life is produced, perceived, and contested.

Of course, this technocapital process carries knock-on effects over the meso-social and individual-micro 'cognitive' levels of human actors. As such, corporations embodying, (re)producing and developing new technologies operate as a locus of production for linked technocapitalism: the practice of advancing science and technology so interconnected with capitalist structures that any advances logically replicate these structures near-automatically. To translate this: capitalism operates akin to a corporate DNA: intrinsic and identifiable as a blueprint within each new technological development.

Parallels between both Crombez's and Suarez-Villa's theorising are evident in Rosa's thinking (Rosa, 2010, 2013, Rosa et al., 2017). Rosa revisits the historic conditions underpinning expanding capitalist growth, and deconstructs constraints operating against emancipation, suggesting societies require specific social conditions to maintain capital-replications. Rosa describes this condition-set as *dynamic stabilisation*—this consisting of linked forms of modern valued capital: material growth, technological innovations, coupled with high volumes of cultural innovation. Evaluating this perspective against Crombez and Suarez-Villa, and drawing on Gramscian theory as an interpretive lens (Gramsci, 2011), nexuses of collective growth in these domains construct foundational *hegemonic* conditions that operate as a bedrock for continued capitalist growth and linked social control/acceptance of this status quo as a recognisable marker of positive social progress. As Rosa et al. (2017) later argue, this paradigm (or hegemony vis-à-vis Gramscian theory) is supported and propagated by three further conditions of *dynamism*: socio-economic appropriation, socio-cultural acceleration, and socio-political activation. Similar to foundational notions of L/Acc: left accelerationism[6] (Fisher, 2018, 2020) and

[6] It is important to be clear in the wake of increasing popular media coverage generalising 'accelerationism' that this L/Acc perspective on accelerationist thinking is divorced from links to R/Acc: right-wing motivated accelerationist thinking. While R/Acc seeks to intensify capitalist structuring via numerous exclusory acts to manifest negative and damaging social changes, L/Acc thinking inversely claims to seek to dismantle or 'repurpose' foundational structures of capitalism via temporary 'disassembling/hijacking' of accelerated growth. This serves to theoretically 'overload' and 'reconfigure' existing structuring principles towards a reformulated equal, egalitarian and collectively inclusive future. While some have claimed this L/Acc perspective as 'destructive' and accelerating capitalist-structured systems towards a final collapse, others have argued this description is inverse

subsequent L/Acc analyses which suggest a fractious relationship between sociotechnological capitalist accelerations and the illusory sustainability of these (Gardiner, 2017; Haynes, 2021; Turner, 2019), Rosa et al. (2017) argue that this present structural dynamic stabilisation model both maintains the integrity of existing capitalism and linked technological progression via its accelerating vectors (i.e. being rapidly developing and self-refining), while also ultimately reproducing a compound accelerating timeline of events which threatens to eventually overwhelm and destabilise itself as a paradoxical product of its perpetuation and integrity-preserving mechanisms. Beyond L/Acc theory, these perspectives have been shared by others (Redhead, 2006, 2007) and within select notions of Paul Virilio. This suggests an inescapable link between the difficulties defining late modernity, and *this* moment's obsession with speed/progress (Virilio, 1995, 2006; Virilio & Bratton, 2006). Such tensions present a paradox of modernity, for which, drawing parallels to Beck's work on risk modernity (Beck, 2002, 2009, 2014), Rosa argues signs are readily visible in the multifarious tensions of contemporary society: the financial, political, environmental, and psychosocial life domains (Rosa et al., 2017). Such tensions can be conceptualised as bringing the technocapitalist hegemony into a threat of *decline*: overwhelmed and placed under threat by its own momentum and replication circuitry.

Although Fisher and others have begun to map the capitalism-technology-anxiety nexus, subsequent scholarship has only partially advanced the conceptual language needed to grasp its contemporary form. The remainder of this work builds on existing foundations but offers a distinct contribution: it draws together adjacent theoretical strands to clarify how collective anxiety is generated and sustained within these structures. In doing so, it develops a unique lens for understanding anxiety as a systemic feature of ***immediate modernity***. I now define this concept directly.

to the goals of L/Acc scholars. For an overview of L/Acc and its contradictions see Gordon (2021), Haynes (2021), and Mackay and Avanessian (2014). Additionally, and more recently, new applications of accelerationism (that disrupt the above descriptive binaries) have evolved.

2.2 Immediate Modernity: Application of Terminology

I employ the term *immediate modernity* to refer to the present—**this**—moment in contemporary Western society: a collective zeitgeist or *contemporary culture ghost*. *This* moment, *immediate modernity*, is defined by the rapid rise and parallel triangular occurrence of three cultural objects: **One/** The interconnected and enduring presence of a pervasive form of hypernormalised[7] capitalism linked to technology. **Two/** Accelerated, ongoing and increasing technological advances, manifesting primarily in digitally heightened and novel ways of connecting human actors together, and connecting single actors to wider social, local, and macro-global events from which they are functionally geographically distanced, but for which new significance and relation are conjured, explicitly via these digital forms of connection. **Three/** A near all-pervasive and heightened form of collective and normalised anxiety, operating as a disruptive and dysfunctional construct to human functioning. Anxiety is positioned both as a natural product of technology-capitalism engagements and accelerations, *and* as a de facto baseline for functional existence in contemporary reality. Just as capitalism and technology are hypernormalised as products of *immediate modernity*, so is automatically attached the inexorably inescapable construct of collective anxiety. Anxiety represents a hallmark of cultural engagement and hegemonic subscription for which (drawing on notions of Beck's *risk society*) responsibility is increasingly placed on the individual to accept and deal with (Beck, 2009).

Together these constructs represent an unparalleled *immediacy*: interconnecting a de facto accelerationist advancement of technology, capitalism, and anxiety via complicit hegemonic consent to existing within this architecture. As such, the moniker of *immediate modernity* takes cues from two interconnected threads of lived-reality experience: the normalised, ongoing and forward-facing speedy advancement of the above three linked constructs, which are **all** accelerating, *and* the temporality paradox of situating these in current, *immediately localised*

[7] The term *hypernormalised* is employed here to frame capitalism as cultural hegemony: an unquestioned, accepted ruling construct that operates as a primary structuring principle over lived existence (Gramsci, 2011).

reality. To clarify, the realist context of the containing culture of *immediate modernity* is itself reactively and repeatedly reconfiguring—self-updating—with such frequency that **this moment** will inevitably be historic as soon as the attachment is coined as *immediate*. Thus, the ability to orient *this moment* in history becomes problematic. Cultural context and its components are accelerating too rapidly to accurately place a marker, pause and reflect, or accurately plot, predict, or reliably track a forward trajectory. As such, while *immediate modernity* refers to the immediately present temporality, it now also refers to the past: the present temporality and its associated linked technological, capitalist and anxiety agendas have now already accelerated beyond this given timestamp at the point of the term being conjured. *Immediate modernity* is employed to describe a social reality in such flux and functional self-replicating state that the *immediate modernity* descriptor, while useful in terms of giving language to this unique temporality, becomes also a paradoxical product of obsolescence as soon as it is attached. This is the unique and specific nature of *immediate modernity*, for *immediate modernity* is both **immediately contemporary** and **immediately obsolete**.

References

Bagby, R. M., Ryder, A. G., Schuller, D. R., & Marshall, M. B. (2004). The Hamilton depression rating scale: Has the gold standard become a lead weight? *American Journal of Psychiatry, 161*(12), 2163–2177. https://doi.org/10.1176/appi.ajp.161.12.2163

Beck, A. T., Epstein, N., Brown, G., & Steer, R. (1993). Beck anxiety inventory. *Journal of Consulting and Clinical Psychology*. [Database Record].

Beck, U. (2002). The terrorist threat: World risk society revisited. *Theory, culture & society, 19*(4), 39–55.

Beck, U. (2009). *World at risk*. Polity.

Beck, U. (2014). *Ulrich Beck: Pioneer in cosmopolitan sociology and risk society*. Springer.

Berardi, F. (2011). *After the future*. AK press.

Crombez, J. M. (2018). *The anxiety and the ecstasy of technical vertigo: Psychological and sociological foundations of critical Socioanalysis from the Italian renaissance to the 21st century* (Doctoral dissertation). University of Tennessee.

Crombez, J. M. (2021). *Anxiety, modern society, and the critical method: Toward a theory and practice of critical socioanalysis* (Vol. 182). Brill.

Deleuze, G. (1992). Postscript on the societies of control. *Cultural theory: An anthology, 59*, 139–142.

Deleuze, G., & Guattari, F. (1972). *Anti-Oedipus: Capitalism and schizophrenia*. University of Minnesota Press.
Deleuze, G., & Guattari, F. (1982). *A thousand plateaus: Capitalism and schizophrenia*. University of Minnesota Press.
Fisher, M. (2014a). *Ghosts of my life: Writings on depression, hauntology and lost futures*. John Hunt Publishing.
Fisher, M. (2014b). Good for nothing. *The Occupied Times.*. https://theoccupiedtimes.org/?p=12841
Fisher, M. (2017). *The weird and the eerie*. Watkins Media Limited.
Fisher, M. (2018). *K-punk: The collected and unpublished writings of mark Fisher (2004–2016)*. Repeater.
Fisher, M. (2020). *Postcapitalist desire: The final lectures*. Watkins Media Limited.
Fisher, M. (2022a). *Capitalist realism: Is there no alternative?* John Hunt Publishing.
Fisher, M. (2022b). *Ghosts of my life: Writings on depression, hauntology and lost futures*. John Hunt Publishing.
Freud, S. (2018). The uncanny. *Dialogues in Philosophy, Mental & Neuro Sciences, 11*(2).
Fullana, M. A., & Shackman, A. J. (2023). Introduction to the special issue on the neurobiology of human fear and anxiety. *Neuroscience & Biobehavioral Reviews, 152*, 105308. https://doi.org/10.1016/j.neubiorev.2023.105308
Gardiner, M. E. (2017). Critique of accelerationism. *Theory, Culture & Society, 34*(1), 29–52.
Giffort, D. (2022). Review of *unnerved: Anxiety, social change, and the transformation of modern mental health. Social Forces, 100*(4), e9. https://doi.org/10.1093/sf/soab155
Gordon, P. (2021). Left accelerationism, transhumanism and the dialectic: Three manifestos. *New Proposals: Journal of Marxism and Interdisciplinary Inquiry, 12*(1), 140–154.
Gramsci, A. (2011). *Prison Notebooks, Volumes 1–3*. Columbia University Press.
Haynes, P. (2021). Is there a future for accelerationism? *Journal of Organizational Change Management, 34*(6), 1175–1187.
Horwitz, A. V. (2013). *Anxiety: A short history*. JHU Press.
Kenwood, M. M., Kalin, N. H., & Barbas, H. (2022). The prefrontal cortex, pathological anxiety, and anxiety disorders. *Neuropsychopharmacology, 47*(1), 260–275.
Land, N. (1993). Machinic desire. *Textual Practice, 7*(3), 471–482.
Land, N. (2009). *'Hyperstition': An introduction*. Delphi Carstens Interviews Nick Land. https://www.orphandriftarchive.com/articles/hyperstition-an-introduction/
Lacan, J. (1988). *The seminar of Jacques Lacan: Book 1: Freud's papers on technique 1953–1954*. CUP Archive.

Land, N. (2012). *Fanged Noumena: Collected writings 1987–2007*. Urbanomic.
Land, N. (2017). A quick-and-dirty introduction to accelerationism. *Jacobite Magazine.*. https://web.archive.org/web/20180113012817/https://jacobitemag.com/2017/05/25/a-quick-and-dirty-introduction-to-accelerationism/
Lee, H. J., & Stein, M. B. (2023). Update on treatments for anxiety-related disorders. *Current Opinion in Psychiatry, 36*(2), 140–145.
Mackay, R., & Avanessian, A. (Eds.). (2014). *# Accelerate: The accelerationist reader*. MIT Press.
NHS. (2022). *Generalised anxiety disorder in adults*. https://www.nhs.uk/mental-health/conditions/generalised-anxiety-disorder/overview/
Nigmatullina, K., & Rodossky, N. (2022). Social media engagement anxiety: Triggers in news agenda. In *International conference on human-computer interaction* (pp. 345–357). Springer.
Rafter, D. (2001). Biochemical markers of anxiety and depression. *Psychiatry Research, 103*(1), 93–96.
Redhead, S. (2006). The art of the accident: Paul Virilio and accelerated modernity. *Fast Capitalism, 2*(1), 1–2.
Redhead, S. (2007). Those absent from the stadium are always right: Accelerated culture, sport media, and theory at the speed of light. *Journal of Sport and Social Issues, 31*(3), 226–241.
Rosa, H. (Ed.). (2010). *High-speed society: Social acceleration, power, and modernity*. Penn State Press.
Rosa, H. (2013). *Social acceleration: A new theory of modernity*. Columbia University Press.
Rosa, H., Dörre, K., & Lessenich, S. (2017). Appropriation, activation and acceleration: The escalatory logics of capitalist modernity and the crises of dynamic stabilization. *Theory, Culture & Society, 34*(1), 53–73.
Shri, R. (2010). Anxiety: Causes and management. *The Journal of Behavioral Science, 5*(1), 100–118.
Smail, D. (2018a). *The origins of unhappiness: A new understanding of personal distress*. Routledge.
Smail, D. (2018b). *Taking care: An alternative to therapy*. Routledge.
Smail, D. (2018c). *Illusion and reality: The meaning of anxiety*. Routledge.
Suarez-Villa, L. (2001). The rise of technocapitalism. *Science & Technology Studies, 14*(2), 4–20.
Suarez-Villa, L. (2003). The e-economy and the rise of technocapitalism: Networks, firms, and transportation. *Growth and Change, 34*(4), 390–414.
Suarez-Villa, L. (2012). *Technocapitalism: A critical perspective on technological innovation and corporatism*. Temple University Press.
Suarez-Villa, L. (2013). *Globalization and technocapitalism: The political economy of corporate power and technological domination*. Ashgate Publishing Ltd.

Tanaka, M., & Chen, C. (2023). Towards a mechanistic understanding of depression, anxiety, and their comorbidity: Perspectives from cognitive neuroscience. *Frontiers in Behavioral Neuroscience, 17*. https://doi.org/10.3389/fnbeh.2023.1268156

Turner, F. (2019). On accelerationism. In *Think in public: A public books reader* (pp. 11–22). Columbia University Press.

Virilio, P. (1995). Speed and information: Cyberspace alarm! *Ctheory, 18*(3), 8–27.

Virilio, P. (2006). *Negative horizon: An essay in dromoscopy*. Bloomsbury Publishing.

Virilio, P., & Bratton, B. H. (2006). *Speed and politics*. MIT Press.

CHAPTER 3

Anxiety Accelerationism: Immediate Capital for Immediate Modernity

For my part, I travel not to go anywhere, but to go. I travel for travel's sake. The great affair is to move; to feel the needs and hitches of our life more nearly; to come down off this feather-bed of civilization, and find the globe granite underfoot and strewn with cutting flints.
Robert Louis Stevenson (1879, Travels with a Donkey in the Cévennes)

Iggy Pop looks right at me as he sings the line: 'America takes drugs in psychic defence'; only he changes 'America' for 'Scatlin', and defines us mair accurately in a single sentence than all the others have ever done.
Irvine Welsh (1993, Trainspotting)

Abstract This chapter explores the affective climate of *immediate modernity*: anxiety. Under technocapital, acceleration has ceased to signify liberation and now represents a grammar of regulation. Drawing from Fisher, Beck and others, this chapter explores how regulation is no longer resisted by capital but absorbed into it, materialising an ambient architecture of control. Accelerationism is reframed as a failed escape route: one that capital has metabolised into a means of managing affect, attention, and time. Anxiety, then, is not a symptom, but a structuring principle of immediate capital.

Keywords Collective anxiety · Accelerationism · Affect · *Immediate modernity*

N. N. Adams, *Terminal Destruction*,
https://doi.org/10.1007/978-3-032-22274-9_3

As introduced in Chapter 2, anxiety in immediate Western society is characterised in individualist terms as an experiential emotion of inner turmoil and discomfort linked to uncertainty, rumination, dread, and unease (APA, 2015; Crocq, 2022). Despite anxious experiences usually triggering functional modifications to social behaviours, anxiety is depicted near-ubiquitously in late modernity as a 'disorder', with 'excessive' presentations linked to negative experiences, psychological ruminations, and mental processing of past, present or future situations (APA, 2015). However, anxiety, when divorced from its disordered framing, represents at a functional, behavioural level an evolutionary construct. It can manifest as a beneficial trait, representing a base human emotion, necessary for survival, and historically understood as reactive to processing and assessment of one's immediate environment and objects existing within: a catalyst for developing processes to keep the individual safe (Bateson et al., 2011; Price, 2013).

Most current theorising with regards to conceptualising 'anxiety disorders' acknowledges anxiety as a relatively commonplace experience for many social actors in modern society (Fullana & Shackman, 2023; Lee & Stein, 2023; Tanaka & Chen, 2023). But, conceptions are rarely linked in literatures to maladjustments triggered by wider rapid macro-societal and technical shifts. Instead, anxiety is routinely suggested as a deviation from 'normal' human thinking, processing, and reacting. This stance is understandable in part. To clarify: the individualistic labelling of anxiety allows for (theoretically) each anxiety-case to be assessed and treated with a degree of individual-centred thinking: the treatment of each human actor as a complex individual with intersecting, manifold social experiences, cognition, and understandings. However, this stance sits somewhat dichotomic with approved, clinically normalised treatments for anxiety. Counselling and psychological therapies are commonly suggested as individualised treatments; but, these follow standardised frameworks for behavioural and cognitive modifications (Heimberg, 2002). Saliently, this standardisation is also seen in uniformed diagnostic metrics for anxiety, such as the Beck Anxiety Inventory (BAI) (Beck et al., 1993). Scales are administered individually to judge personal anxiety experience, but scales are scored per centrally set questions and benchmarks, and these are formalised from established population 'norms'. This standardisation extends to approved anxiety medications, which while undoubtedly essential and life-saving, function by initiating neurological chemical alterations that approximate bio-emulation of cognitive anxiolytic states. Their effects are determined by standardised clinical trial 'successes'. Such compounds are not synthesised to illicit anxiety-mitigating effects bespoke to the individual sufferer based on their experience, perception or sensemaking of anxiety catalysts, but instead, to achieve the goal of anxiety-mitigation within and across the widest possible demographic, to ensure prescriptions represent a normalised offering, with the highest overall success potential and least side effect prevalence (Allgulander, 1999; Bandelow et al., 2022; Blanco et al., 2003; Fullana & Shackman, 2023).

David Smail (2018a, 2018b) provides a conceptual lens here that complements macro-level theorising of anxiety, when framed through Beck's (2002, 2009, 2014) work on reflexive *risk society* and Rosa's (2010, 2013) conceptions of social acceleration. Smail (like Fisher) does not situate anxiety as a cognitive malfunction, but a meaningful response to socio-structural pressures/constraints. Anxiety is neither arbitrary nor inherently pathological: it signals the tensions produced by social, technological, and economic systems, the same networked constructs that I argue define *immediate modernity*. Smail (2018a) likewise critiques the clinical focus on symptom reduction, arguing therapeutic frameworks often obscure wider structural causes in favour of treating anxious manifestations. In alignment with Beck and Rosa, anxiety can thus represent a barometer of the relational and material world, spotlighting insights into how social, technological, and economic forces condition human perception of safety, agency, and belonging. This perspective situates individualised interventions, whether standardised therapy or pharmacological solutions, within a broader social context, highlighting the dissonance between collective sources of anxiety and individually targeted treatments.

To this end then, *immediate modernity*'s anxiety conceptualisations are acutely dichotomic. While anxiety appears on the one hand to be recognised as collective and wide-ranging in prevalence and effect, anxiety is concurrently diagnosed and made sense of as an individual malfunction, positioned as caused by specific psychosocial and neurological alterations. Despite this, treatments are developed to be applicable on a macro-collective as opposed to individualistic scale, yet readily offered as reactive solutions to anxiety as an individually-labelled problem. This is despite evidence spotlighting the importance of understanding collective societal contributions and causes of anxiety (Bateson et al., 2011; Crombez, 2021; Rosa et al., 2017; Suarez-Villa, 2013).

3.1 Anxiety as a Reaction to Sociotechnical Accelerations

Additional scholarships also divorce from viewing anxiety in individualistic terms. Studies explore collective anxiety increases as reactionary to rapid social changes. Just as total individual perspectives are inadequate, these works require exploration and evaluation. Locating this thinking within an *immediate modernity* context, theorising can be broken down into three interlinked topic areas:

(one) humans coping with the unpredictable risks of rapid techno-social accelerations;
(two) social actors developing sensemaking regarding rapid technological developments and their effects upon social interactions; and.
(three) sensemaking surrounding future technological accelerations and their probable effects on humans and society.

Ulrich Beck's work on reflexivity and risk modernity is perhaps some of the most cited scholarship linking radical social change and anxiety. Collectively Beck's notions are reactive to the ideas of postmodernity. Namely, that modernity has a natural, clarifying endpoint with regard to techno-social advances. For example, the notion that modernity concludes in the 1980–1990s and postmodernity, and its associated new advances, subsequently begins with a 'clean slate' (Jameson, 1991). Reactive to this, Beck's work explores *reflexive modernity*, a concept prioritising the recognition of rising individuality and displacement of power following the achievement of modernity's ideals (Beck, 2009, 2014). Central to Beck's theories are acknowledgements of the aftereffect 'risks' unintentionally constructed by past advances. Beck labels this social temporality 'reflexive', indicating a need for society as an ever-growing individualistic construct to shift to a united collective-reflexivity perspective. This is to approach the development of solutions to the now pre-existing risks of *immediate modernity*, for example: climate change, nuclear engineering, biotechnology. These notions are situated alongside a second theoretical branch: Beck's work on *risk society* (Beck, 2002, 2014). Theory focusses on deconstructing the ways in which immediately modern society arranges in response to risk, using risk to structure and make sense of insecurities unintentionally introduced by past modernisations, but which must now be addressed, solved, and dealt with in present *immediate modernity* alongside *immediate modernity*'s own natural techno-social advances and the additional compound risks created by these (e.g. artificial intelligence, social fragmentation, global pandemics). As society remains preoccupied with solving past risk problems, while generating both new technologies and striving to mitigate any additional risks conjured, society itself begins to become collectively preoccupied with risk, using this framing as a structuring principle for self-examination, social sensemaking, individualist cognitive processing and a template for social, financial, and technological interactions (Beck, 2014; Beck et al., 1992).

Fredric Jameson's theorising complicates this 'risk' landscape further. For Jameson (1991), late capitalism accelerates, but also reorganises social processes; reconfiguring the structures of perceptual experience. Temporal depth collapses, historical continuity fragments, and culture becomes dominated by simulation, recycling, and stylistic pastiche. This temporal flattening generates characteristic affects: disorientation, suspended agency, and an inability to locate oneself within broader trajectories of social change. Crucially, Jameson argues that late-capitalist acceleration is not just a matter of rapid change but of temporal enclosure: a cultural logic that traps subjects inside an ever-intensifying (and increasingly uncertain) present. When read alongside Beck, Jameson's argument clarifies how anxiety emerges not only from proliferating risks but from the concurrent erosion of temporal stability itself, a core dynamic of *immediate modernity*. In what follows, I apply these lenses to explore how sociotechnical accelerations manifest across everyday digital life. First, I examine how intensified communication infrastructures reorganise subjectivity into the dividual. Second, I explore how social media amplifies anxiety through cycles of fragmentation, judgement, and comparison. Third, I trace how disaster-oriented media circulates global risk at overwhelming speeds. Finally, I spotlight anxieties emerging from technological failure, corruption, and AI-driven uncertainty, revealing how networked accelerations destabilise selfhood, agency, and imaginaries of the future.

3.2 Anxiety Arising from Digital Communication Technology

Numerous ghosts of Beck's 'unintended risk' theorising are readily uncovered when interrogating modern scholarship, particularly with regards to changed interaction trends and communication technology. The following analysis, invoking deterritorialisation and reterritorialisation, establishes conceptual groundwork for understanding how subjectivity is reorganised within *immediate modernity*. As signposted in Chapter 2, dividualisation refers to the process through which the coherent, autonomous individual is decomposed into divisible units of data, behaviour, and affect. Importantly, this condition precedes the advent of social media and should be understood as a longer historical tendency within technocapitalism, traceable through earlier material, linguistic, and economic mediations. But, under the conditions of *immediate modernity*, subjectivity is no longer stable or self-contained but distributed across the digitised networks and systems through which it is made most productive. Interactive technologies intensify this pre-existing process rather than originate it, amplifying and aestheticising the forms of psychic and social fragmentation already latent within modernity. Contemporary digital infrastructures therefore exacerbate specific symptoms and modes of reterritorialisation, rendering the dividual more visible as a dominant configuration of technocapitalist life. The dividual emerges here as the figure through which these forces converge: neither liberated from nor fully determined by technocapital's circuits, yet perpetually modulated within them. It is through this framing that the following section reconsiders the relationship between the 'offline' and 'online' selves, situating digital mediation as an interpretive extension of the Deluzian dividual analysis rather than its chronological origin (Deleuze, 1992; Deleuze & Guattari, 1982).

A study by Pierce (2009) offers an early illustration of how digitally mediated communication reshapes anxiety in younger users. Pierce found that teens increasingly rely on SIT (Socially Interactive Technologies), such as online messaging and digital mobile communication, and that higher social anxiety in "talk[ing] face to face" (p. 1369) corresponded with greater preference for using SIT-based interactions. Subsequent research supports findings, suggesting that digital mediation is becoming a preferred mode of human interaction, functioning as an anxiety buffer in *immediate modernity* (Gabbiadini et al., 2020;

Indwar & Mishra, 2022). Yet this sits alongside an opposite body of work linking heightened digital communication with increased anxiety and psychological strain (Bartlett, 2017; Cain, 2018; Nieminen, 2016). Rosen et al. (2013) highlight this contradiction directly: their work on Facebook use demonstrates various associations among social media activity volume, number of online friends, and symptoms of psychiatric disorders, while simultaneously noting perceived benefits of online engagement. Beyond communication patterns, studies also signpost deeper shifts in how social actors understand and value themselves. The locus of affirmation increasingly moves from the tangible-physical realm to the virtual, where self-perception and self-worth become tied to the volume, rhythm, and temporality of receiving or not receiving 'likes' (Di Gesto et al., 2023; Mackson et al., 2019; Mullin, 2017; Vander Dussen, 2021). This intersects with research tracing anxieties around appearance and self-presentation (Amoda et al., 2022; Bue, 2020; Seekis & Kennedy, 2023). Additional studies further identify social media 'likes' as a key mediator of perceived real-world anxiety and self-esteem (Burrow & Rainone, 2017; Lee et al., 2020; Reich et al., 2023), underscoring how digital realities feedback into 'offline' psychological states.

Synthesising evidence, psychological and sociological scholarship pinpoints that social actors build their sense of self through the perceived judgements of others (Goffman, 2002; Niedenthal et al., 2005; Scheff, 2005). Cooley's (1902) *looking-glass self* formalises this: individuals form self-images by interpreting others' responses, and by anticipating how they believe others evaluate them (Hensley, 1996). In *immediate modernity*, however, this interpersonal dynamic becomes technologically mediated. Self-worth is increasingly anchored in the presentation of curated digital fragments: *selective snapshots* uploaded for evaluation within tightly bounded virtual environments. This produces a cycle of judgement and readjustment, intensified by the architecture of platforms designed to reward visibility and curation. Crucially, actors become conditioned to edit their digital self-presentations to foreground only those 'spectres' or shadows of identity most likely to attract positive virtual appraisal. In some cases, these judgements are sought from audiences the individual has never met offline, yet whose *virtual capital—high* follower counts, network visibility—grants them disproportionate influence. This curatorial logic ranges from selective posting of images and 'stories' to more active manipulation of self-representation using built-in mobile filters and editing tools (Ibsen et al., 2022). At the more extreme, applications such as Facetune enable granular alteration of skin tone, facial proportions, contouring, and other physical features (Bahnweg & Omar, 2023; Ellis & Destine, 2023). These practices crystallise a central tension of ***immediate modernity***: identity becomes something spliced, filtered, and aestheticised for external consumption, with the virtual 'avatar' increasingly mediating if not eclipsing the embodied self as a perceived representation of 'true' identity.

Contemporary digital interactions sharpen an acute risk-orientation towards virtual communication. Returning to the role of 'likes': these operate as digital proxies for approval, functioning much like Cooley's *looking-glass self* by signalling symbolic appraisal of the curated, virtually shared image (Burrow & Rainone, 2017; Di Gesto et al., 2023; Lee et al., 2020). Yet the image being judged is often a modified or digitally enhanced version of the actor: a stratified offering that diverges from their embodied appearance. This produces a corrosive drift of the looking-glass: digital mediation inserts an interpretive layer that fractures the reflective loop. What is judged is not the 'self' but a synthetic, curated proxy. This generates a triadic comparison structure particular to today's digital society. Actors assess not only others' judgements of the uploaded fragment but also the distance between that fragment and their own unaltered, imperfect baseline. Digital tools enable the presentation of an 'idealised self', but if that idealisation is judged harshly, the implications for subsequent self-evaluation are intensified. Conversely, even favourable judgements bind affirmation to a version of self that may be only loosely connected to the actor's embodied identity. Consequently, every digital communication, whether an image, a post, or a short textual interaction, invokes a form of risk assessment. Social media platforms render such exchanges inherently judgement-oriented, reducing their social currency to the collective metric of 'likes'. The result is a communicative economy where affirmation and anxiety are tightly coupled, each interaction reinforcing the precariousness of being evaluated through fragments rather than through the whole self.

These dynamics extend into the micro-politics of following and unfollowing, and the quiet metrics of social visibility. The absence of a 'like', the loss of a follower or connection, or a sudden drop in engagement acquires disproportionate affective weight. These small digital signals, often ambiguous, accidental, or incidental, are read as totalising social verdicts. Actors may experience anxiety when posts are ignored, when someone disconnects without explanation, or when a previously responsive audience turns silent. Such fluctuations are interpreted not as routine digital instabilities but as judgements on the curated fragment of self placed into circulation. In this way, platform metrics become interpretive cues through which individuals attempt to gauge their social standing, desirability, or legitimacy. The result is a low-grade relational vigilance, continually sustained by architectures that make digital self-presentation both inevitable and emotionally consequential.

Under *immediate modernity*, the subject no longer appears as a coherent individual but as a *dividual*—a being decomposed into discrete, circulating fragments of data, affect, and presentation. Social media intensifies this condition by requiring actors to present themselves in slices. Each uploaded fragment becomes a unit of dividualised selfhood offered for judgement. Actors share these fragments knowing the process is inherently risky. Positive judgement delivers only momentary validation of the fragment, not of the whole self. Negative judgement, conversely, prompts doubt about the fragment's social acceptability and may lead to its suppression in future presentations. Even when feedback is positive, a dissonance emerges: the fragment being validated is rarely congruent with the actor's fuller, offline self. It is an edited motif the actor anticipates will be most acceptable to the virtual collective. Thus, even genuine posts function as spectral shadows: condensed slivers of identity whose validation is fragile and temporary. Because the dividual self is distributed across these fragments, actors are compelled to repeat the cycle: share another slice, await judgement, recalibrate, and present again. The platform logic demands continual fragmentary disclosure, each submission reactivating the same risk calculus. Over time, this produces frustration, as actors recognise they are constrained to a thin, reductive sampling of the human condition: a narrow bandwidth of selfhood optimised for platform visibility rather than lived coherence. Where fragments are idealised through digital enhancement, positive judgement introduces yet another tension: the pressure to bring the offline body into congruence with the virtual *avatar*. This gap between the machinically optimised representation and the embodied self becomes a further site of anxiety. The dividual is thus pulled between incompatible demands: accurate self-expression, socially acceptable fragments, and platform-driven idealisation, with each intensifying the psychic strain generated by *immediate modernity*'s accelerated systems of visibility, evaluation, and self-production.

Conceptualising this process in macro-level terms, we may ask the question:

Following collective uptake in this virtual communication trend, can social actors ever be whole?— given the normalised social importance placed on the sharing and judgement of fractured spectres of social identity in the realm of the virtual and the tendency to manipulate these sharings towards self and group perceptions of a perceived virtual ideal.

Before closing this point, it is important to note that much of the existing research focuses on the negative effects of digital self-manipulation on women (Bue, 2020; Seekis & Kennedy, 2023), though men are also shown to be affected (Fatt et al., 2019). The concentration of studies on women is difficult to attribute to a single causal factor. While some evidence suggests women may engage with certain platforms or practices differently than men (Krasnova et al., 2017), extrapolating broad claims from such patterns risks reinscribing gender generalisations and flattening the substantial variation within and between female-identifying groups, post-constructivist identities, and intersecting femininities. Equally, men may be comparably affected but are less likely to report or disclose distress surrounding appearance, self-presentation, or technologised self-comparison. This under-visibility should not be read as absence of impact but as an artefact of hegemonic masculinity, where cultural norms still position discussions of vulnerability, appearance anxiety, or self-doubt as inversions of masculine legitimacy (Connell, 2020). Applying an intersectional framing to masculinities further complicates the picture: the diversity of masculinised identities is too wide to support singular causal narratives without collapsing important distinctions. Thus, anxiety linked to digital self-manipulation operates across genders, but surfaces through different cultural scripts, silences, and modes of dividualised self-presentation, and the topic requires further interrogation.

3.3 Anxiety and Exposure to 'Disaster News'

Expanding on the above threads of thought, anxiety influences of the virtual transcend beyond direct communicative interaction and engagement. While social actors are often caught in a cyclic perpetuation of virtual validation-seeking, concurrently, socially-focussed technologies also expose individuals to global risks and catastrophes continuously as a hallmark and unintended consequence of technological global connectivity. For example, akin to Beck's work, Ian Wilkinson's scholarship *Anxiety in a risk society* draws linkages between risk-based sensemaking and Western media maintaining a state of urgency crisis: a perpetual and unrelenting fascination with the promotion of threat and insecurity motifs (Wilkinson, 2022). Technological permanence as encouraging risk-focussed thinking is perhaps best exampled via the 'always-on' newsfeeds and second-by-second global updates shared via smartphones, apps, software and almost all interactive technology. This phenomenon runs parallel and connects to the anxieties surrounding fragmented identity sharing on social media.

Evidencing this, Dong and Zheng (2020) explore the impact of headline 'netnews' topics upon the stress levels of 1026 individuals in China, during the Covid-19 outbreak. They highlight "endless reports from news media" (p. 1) can lead to both physical and mental disorders, including "anxiety disorders [and] depression disorders" (p. 1). A similar study by Zhao and Zhou (2020) explored linkages between "Disaster stressor[s]" (p. 1), mental health and social media use in a time of Covid-19. Scholars found higher levels of social media use correlated with worsened mental health. Relatedly, more exposure and interaction with "disaster news" (p. 1) resulted in greater depression for participants. The authors concluded disaster stressors amplify the negative effects of social media use on depression. Perspectives shared from research conducted in other locales reveal similar findings (Fuki & Yoshida, 2015; Kelly & Ahmad, 2014; Madell, 2006; Murdock, 2010; Shabahang et al., 2021).

In *immediate modernity*, social actors are increasingly and unavoidably tethered to global crises far beyond their immediate lifeworld. Disaster media amplifies this saturation: depictions of accidents, risks, and societal breakdown prioritise the most shocking elements to capture attention rather than to offer solutions. This dynamic aligns with Crombez's (2021) account of technological anomie and Rosa's (2010, 2013) "frenetic standstill" (2013, p. 71) where acceleration produces paralysis rather than action. Disaster news thus becomes a normalised signal of collective failure: a continuous warning without any corresponding reflexive pathway, directly countering Beck's vision of a reflexive *risk society* (Beck, 2002, 2009, 2014). At the same time, the virtual circulation of these *disaster stressors* creates a delocalising effect. Just as social media fragments the symbolic self into curated 'bytes', disaster events are reduced to consumable, scrollable units on apps, tablets, and smartphones. This translation can unintentionally soften, aestheticise, or even gamify catastrophe, producing a mediated distance from the 'real' event. Such dynamics echo Suarez-Villa's (2012) account of technocapitalism's digitalising pressures and Fisher's (1999, 2022) concerns regarding technology-driven cultural deterioration and corrupted sensemaking as tragedy becomes increasingly capitalised.

Smail (2018b) further elucidates the paradox of control inherent in contemporary anxiety. Linking with Beck's (2014) notion of reflexive *risk society*, and Rosa's (2010, 2013) argument regarding social acceleration, individuals encounter an abundance of information and technological connectivity that amplifies awareness of systemic risk: ranging from climate change to pandemics, yet provides limited capacity to meaningfully intervene. Disaster news and digital media channels intensify this effect, manufacturing persistent anxiety as a rational response to structural realities. Fisher's (1999, 2017, 2018) work on technological unease resonates here, highlighting the uncanny tension between human actors and artificial or digitally-mediated constructs, further complicating the perception of control. Per Smail's perspective, the anxiety arising in these contexts is intelligible: it reflects a confrontation with forces that exceed personal agency, yet social conditioning encourages individuals to interpret this anxiety as a sign of weakness or internal deficit. Consequently, exposure to disaster news and digital networks exemplifies how anxiety in *immediate modernity* is simultaneously socially produced, technologically mediated, and individually experienced, reinforcing the need to consider structural and systemic interventions alongside individualised therapies.

These dynamics further intensify through increasingly granular forms of technological mediation. For instance, disaster content is now frequently delivered through hyper-targeted systems that read and respond to the dividual traces users leave across platforms. A single search or click can trigger a cascade of algorithmically curated crisis material, not because the individual consciously seeks it out, but because their behavioural fragments are recombined into a 'risk-interest profile' that then governs what they are shown. Parallel to this, disaster events are routinely transformed into spectacles of engagement, where livestreamed crises accumulate reaction metrics: viewer counts, comment velocities, trending indices, that function as their own secondary drama. Here, catastrophe becomes a site of performativity: users may feel compelled to remain informed, to respond, to participate in the circulating affect, as if their relevance is tied to their vigilance. This is further complicated by the emergence of hyperreal proximities, in which individuals encounter high-definition footage, drone feeds, and instantaneous reportage from events occurring continents away, collapsing spatial distance and producing an unnervingly intimate encounter with crises they cannot meaningfully intervene in. The cumulative effect is a form of *algorithmic empathy fatigue*: an emotional blunting coupled with physiological activation, where users become caught in a continuous low-grade state of anxiety. This is not the outcome of personal fragility but the structural consequence of technocapitalist exposure: anxiety produced by systems that exceed agency, interpret behaviour in divisible units, and feed those fragments back into experience as if they were the individual's own desire. As such, social actors live in constant proximity to disaster through technological mediation, yet are simultaneously distanced from its material reality. This produces a persistent dissonance: risk feels omnipresent, but abstracted, visible as a stream of curated, aestheticised crisis images that can be dismissed with a single swipe. Disaster becomes both hyper-present and strangely out of focus. This virtual lens fractures the two dynamics Beck saw as indispensable to reflexive *risk society*: a recognition of collective failure (*what have we done?*) and a sense of collective responsibility. Instead, the virtual substitutes the latter with a quiet but pervasive *there is nothing you can do*. The result is a paradox of agency: users feel overwhelmed by crisis yet structurally positioned as spectators, not actors. The apparent control offered by digital interfaces, the ability to close an app or silence an alert, is largely illusory. Like the curated fragments of self, shared on social media, disaster content is consumed in addictive, normalised cycles. And in both cases, the interaction produces the same effect: an intensifying inertia, where awareness deepens but the capacity to intervene contracts. Anxiety accumulates not despite this dynamic but because of it, accelerating alongside the very systems that deliver it.

3.4 Anxieties from Technological Failures, Corruptions, and Uncertain Future Accelerations

Alongside concerns surrounding technological failures, *immediate modernity* generates a parallel anxiety, one rooted in technologies that accelerate beyond their intended uses, producing forms of arbitration, simulation, and influence that outpace actors' ability to interpret or contain them. Social actors experience anxiety when technologies become *corrupted*, either through the unintended consequences of rapid technological acceleration or through their repurposing beyond their original scope. Empirical studies show that even brief disruptions in smartphone availability can elicit measurable distress (Cheever et al., 2014; Lin et al., 2017; Tams et al., 2018; Van Den Eijnden et al., 2017). In some cases, the mere *possibility* of unavailability is enough to provoke anxiety, reflecting fears of disconnection, loss of communicative continuity, and missing out on social or global events. These responses point to a deeper structural dependency: technologies do not simply mediate experience, they scaffold the rhythms through which actors feel socially, emotionally, and informationally anchored. A related and rapidly expanding body of scholarship examines anxieties that arise not from technological breakdowns but from technological *excess*: AI systems, Deepfakes, AI video content, and virtual agents capable of simulating human affect with increasing fidelity. Research identifies a persistent unease or distrust surrounding these developments (Cover, 2022; Rajaobelina et al., 2021). These concerns cluster around two broad arenas. First, actors experience dissonance when interacting with virtual constructs that appear almost, but not quite, human, generating feelings of uncanniness and destabilisation. Second, anxieties extend towards the future: worries about what continued techno-advancements might mean for human identity, agency, and autonomy, and how these systems may evolve beyond their intended contours. Together, these dynamics illustrate how anxieties emerge not only when technologies fail, but also when they succeed too well, exceeding familiar parameters and unsettling established distinctions between the human, the machinic, and the social.

Fisher's work on the unease surrounding *flatline constructs* is instructive here (Fisher, 1999, 2017). Borrowing Gibson's figure of *the flatline* from *Neuromancer*[1] (Gibson, 1984), Fisher foregrounds Dixie Flatline: a copied human consciousness that persists only as ROM, no longer *alive* yet still interactively present. In *Neuromancer* Case's encounters with Dixie generate a distinctive discomfort: Dixie convincingly mimics affect, memory, and conversational rhythm, yet this performance sits in tension with the knowledge that the 'person' behind it is dead. The result is an uncanny oscillation between recognition and estrangement, a profoundly affective disturbance produced by something that is neither fully human

[1] A novel by William Gibson.

nor fully machine. My own reading of Fisher extends this dynamic beyond fiction: *immediate modernity* increasingly stages comparable forms of unease as AI systems accelerate in sophistication (Fisher, 1999, 2017, 2018). The dead/undead dichotomy becomes less a metaphor and more a diagnostic register for understanding these encounters. Contemporary systems emulate affect, tone, and human expressivity with startling fidelity, yet always retain machinic seams: gaps, glitches, or overcompensated performances that unsettle the interaction. These moments fracture the symbolic boundary between life and non-life, producing precisely the kind of uncanny tension Fisher locates in Dixie (Fisher, 1999). From this perspective, traditional categories of the 'alive' and the 'dead' begin to lose coherence in environments where simulation, replication, and technical persistence continually blur their distinction. Chapter 9 develops this argument fully, analysing how immersive videogames and media technologies amplify this *flatline* uncanny as a defining experiential texture of contemporary technoculture.

As per some emerging literatures (Cover, 2022), unease experienced when interacting with AI constructs is primarily resultant of actors' inability to immediately differentiate the AI construct from a human. As Fisher (1999) alludes to, unease is also at times experienced when actors perceive something 'slightly off' about the human mimicry elements of AI technology, perhaps, notions that AI constructs are 'overly emulating' specific components of human interaction in ways real human-users perceive as unnatural, while concurrently under-emulating other human traits, vocal mannerisms, and behaviours. Such unease-markers allow AI technologies to 'pass' for human, but at the cost of high levels of unease and 'uncanny' notions experienced by the human actor interacting with the AI construct. This primarily manifests as a sense of psychological unease: an experience of *the uncanny* (see Fisher, 1999[2]).

A second cluster of anxieties concerns the broader implications of accelerating AI development. Here the unease is less about specific interactions and more about what such systems threaten to erode: human identity, individuality, and the sense of being irreplaceably *human*. Fears about the trajectory of AI intelligence, whether it will surpass, destabilise, or simply

[2] *The uncanny* is discussed most directly beginning on pages 4, 115, and 163 within Fisher, (1999).

outpace human capacities, generate a pervasive ambiguity about the technical future. Questions surrounding a possible technological singularity,[3] and whether its outcomes would be utopian or dystopian, sit alongside more localised worries vis-à-vis the everyday blurring of boundaries between human and machine. These concerns also manifest socially: uncertainty over whether one can reliably distinguish AI 'assistants' from human interlocutors, anxiety about which occupations may be displaced, and doubt over the wisdom of outsourcing key social processes to algorithmic systems. Early evidence suggests this anxiety is already taking shape in online settings, with interactions increasingly tinged by suspicion or discomfort. Correspondingly, the term *automation anxiety* has emerged to capture fears surrounding the potential loss of role, purpose, or employment to machine-based systems (Baek et al., 2022).

3.5 Summary

The preceding sections extend existing scholarship on the capitalism–technology–anxiety nexus by clarifying how human actors in *immediate modernity* inhabit a dense technological environment that reorganises selfhood, attention, and affect. Social currency has shifted decisively towards the virtual: interaction and self-worth are routed through platforms that fragment identity into curated slices. While communication technologies reduce physical distance, they simultaneously restructure the value of human interaction, normalising a dividual mode of selfhood in which actors present optimised fragments for continual judgement. This drives cycles of self-comparison, dissonance, and unstable validation tethered to synthetic, often digitally altered, images of the self. Alongside this micro-level fragmentation sits an intensified macro-level exposure to global crises. Disaster media renders risk ever-present yet materially remote, saturating daily life with aestheticised catastrophe that can be dismissed with a swipe. This produces a paradoxical state where actors feel both hyper-aware of collective failure and structurally unable to intervene. Anxiety emerges not from personal fragility but from the tension between

[3] A hypothetical event where technological growth becomes rapid and uncontrollable, birthing AIs with intelligence beyond that of the humans that created AI. Specifically, the rise of AI Superinteligence and Artificial General Intelligence (AGI) are possible as outcomes of a singularity event. Some interpretations of /Acc theory cite this event as heralding a reformulation of capitalist society structures.

proximity to crisis and the distancing effects of technological mediation. Compounding these dynamics are anxieties tied to technological excess: rapidly advancing AI, Deepfakes, and machinic simulations that unsettle distinctions between the human and the non-human. These developments provoke ontological uncertainty regarding agency, identity, and the future of human uniqueness. Everyday encounters with increasingly sophisticated virtual agents amplify this unease, as technology accelerations blur symbolic boundaries and render familiar categories unstable. Across these domains, anxiety is revealed as opposite to framings of this as an individual disorder, but as a systemic affect produced by the accelerated, fragmenting, and risk-saturated conditions of ***immediate modernity***. Actors are compelled to navigate environments that outpace interpretive capacity, collapse temporal depth, and distribute selfhood across dividual fragments. Anxiety thus becomes the rational affective signature of contemporary technoculture. This analysis lays the groundwork for the next chapter, where I examine how these dynamics intersect with the concept of *the beau idéal disconnect*.

References

Allgulander, C. (1999). Paroxetine in social anxiety disorder: A randomized placebo-controlled study. *Acta Psychiatrica Scandinavica, 100*(3), 193–198. https://doi.org/10.1111/j.1600-0447.1999.tb10845.x

Amoda, M., Domingo, N., Gasgonia, L., & Relleve, C. (2022). Self-esteem and social appearance anxiety of TikTok users: Appraising social support as probable moderator. *International Journal of Scientific Research in Multidisciplinary Studies, 8*(4), 47–51.

APA—American Psychiatric Association. (2015). *Anxiety disorders: DSM-5® selections*. American Psychiatric Publications.

Baek, S. U., Yoon, J. H., & Won, J. U. (2022). Association between workers' anxiety over technological automation and sleep disturbance: Results from a nationally representative survey. *International Journal of Environmental Research and Public Health, 19*(16), 10051. https://doi.org/10.3390/ijerph191610051

Bahnweg, E., & Omar, H. (2023). Effects of TikTok on adolescent mental health and wellbeing. *Dynamics of Human Health, 10*(1). https://journalofhealth.co.nz/?page_id=2905

Bandelow, B., Michaelis, S., & Wedekind, D. (2022). Treatment of anxiety disorders. *Dialogues in Clinical Neuroscience*, 93–107. https://doi.org/10.31887/DCNS.2017.19.2/bbandelow

Bartlett, V. (2017). The double bind effect: Art and anxiety in a digital age. *Art, 37*(3), 34–38.
Bateson, M., Brilot, B., & Nettle, D. (2011). Anxiety: An evolutionary approach. *The Canadian Journal of Psychiatry, 56*(12), 707–715. https://doi.org/10.1177/070674371105601202
Beck, U. (2002). The terrorist threat: World risk society revisited. *Theory, Culture & Society, 19*(4), 39–55.
Beck, U. (2009). *World at risk*. Polity.
Beck, U. (2014). *Ulrich Beck: Pioneer in cosmopolitan sociology and risk society*. Springer.
Beck, A. T., Epstein, N., Brown, G., & Steer, R. (1993). Beck anxiety inventory. *Journal of Consulting and Clinical Psychology* [Database Record].
Beck, U., Lash, S., & Wynne, B. (1992). *Risk society: Towards a new modernity*. Sage.
Blanco, C., Schneier, F. R., Schmidt, A., Blanco-Jerez, C. R., Marshall, R. D., Sánchez-Lacay, A., & Liebowitz, M. R. (2003). Pharmacological treatment of social anxiety disorder: A meta-analysis. *Depression and Anxiety, 18*(1), 29–40. https://doi.org/10.1002/da.10096
Bue, A. C. C. (2020). The looking glass selfie: Instagram use frequency predicts visual attention to high-anxiety body regions in young women. *Computers in Human Behavior, 108*, 106329.
Burrow, A. L., & Rainone, N. (2017). How many likes did I get? Purpose moderates links between positive social media feedback and self-esteem. *Journal of Experimental Social Psychology, 69*, 232–236.
Cain, J. (2018). It's time to confront student mental health issues associated with smartphones and social media. *American Journal of Pharmaceutical Education, 82*(7), 6862.
Cheever, N. A., Rosen, L. D., Carrier, L. M., & Chavez, A. (2014). Out of sight is not out of mind: The impact of restricting wireless mobile device use on anxiety levels among low, moderate and high users. *Computers in Human Behavior, 37*, 290–297.
Connell, R. W. (2020). *Masculinities*. Routledge.
Cooley, C. H. (1902). The looking-glass self. The production of reality: Essays and readings on social interaction, 6(1902), 126–128.
Cover, R. (2022). *Deepfake culture: The emergence of audio-video deception as an object of social anxiety and regulation* (pp. 1–13). Continuum.
Crocq, M. A. (2022). A history of anxiety: From Hippocrates to DSM. *Dialogues in clinical neuroscience*. Taylor & Francis.
Crombez, J. M. (2021). *Anxiety, modern society, and the critical method: Toward a theory and practice of critical socioanalysis* (Vol. 182). Brill.
Deleuze, G. (1992). Postscript on the societies of control. *Cultural theory: An anthology, 59*, 139–142.

Deleuze, G., & Guattari, F. (1982). *A thousand plateaus: Capitalism and schizophrenia*. University of Minnesota Press.

Di Gesto, C., Matera, C., Policardo, G. R., & Nerini, A. (2023). Instagram as a digital mirror: The effects of instagram likes and disclaimer labels on self-awareness, body dissatisfaction, and social physique anxiety among young Italian women. *Current Psychology, 42*(17), 14663–14672.

Dong, M., & Zheng, J. (2020). Headline stress disorder caused by Netnews during the outbreak of COVID-19. *Health Expectations: An International Journal of Public Participation in Health Care and Health Policy, 23*(2), 259–260. https://doi.org/10.1111%2Fhex.13055

Ellis, N. P., & Destine, S. (2023). Color capital: Examining the racialized nature of beauty via colorism and skin bleaching. *Sociology Compass*, e13049.

Fatt, S. J., Fardouly, J., & Rapee, R. M. (2019). # malefitspo: Links between viewing fitspiration posts, muscular-ideal internalisation, appearance comparisons, body satisfaction, and exercise motivation in men. *New Media & Society, 21*(6), 1311–1325.

Fisher, M. (1999). *Flatline constructs: Gothic materialism and cybernetic theory-fiction* (Doctoral dissertation). University of Warwick.

Fisher, M. (2017). *The weird and the eerie*. Watkins Media Limited.

Fisher, M. (2018). *K-punk: The collected and unpublished writings of mark Fisher (2004–2016)*. Repeater.

Fisher, M. (2022). *Capitalist realism: Is there no alternative?* John Hunt Publishing.

Fuki, K., & Yoshida, F. (2015). Mobile phone-related behaviors and problems in Japan. In *Encyclopedia of mobile phone behavior* (pp. 1079–1088). IGI Global.

Fullana, M. A., & Shackman, A. J. (2023). Introduction to the special issue on the neurobiology of human fear and anxiety. *Neuroscience & Biobehavioral Reviews, 152*, 105308. https://doi.org/10.1016/j.neubiorev.2023.105308

Gabbiadini, A., Baldissarri, C., Durante, F., Valtorta, R. R., De Rosa, M., & Gallucci, M. (2020). Together apart: The mitigating role of digital communication technologies on negative affect during the COVID-19 outbreak in Italy. *Frontiers in Psychology, 11*, 554678.

Gibson, W. (1984). *Neuromancer*. Harper Voyager.

Goffman, E. (2002). The presentation of self in everyday life. *Garden City, NY, 259* (1959).

Heimberg, R. G. (2002). Cognitive-behavioral therapy for social anxiety disorder: Current status and future directions. *Biological Psychiatry, 51*(1), 101–108.

Hensley, W. E. (1996). A theory of the valenced other: The intersection of the looking-glass-self and social penetration. *Social Behavior and Personality: An International Journal, 24*(3), 293–308.

Ibsen, M., Rathgeb, C., Fischer, D., Drozdowski, P., & Busch, C. (2022). Digital face manipulation in biometric systems. In *Handbook of digital face manipulation and detection: From DeepFakes to morphing attacks* (pp. 27–43). Springer.

Indwar, R. G., & Mishra, A. S. (2022). Emojis: Can it reduce post-purchase dissonance? *Journal of Strategic Marketing, 31*, 1–22.

Jameson, F. (1991). *Postmodernism, or, the cultural logic of late capitalism*. Duke University Press.

Kelly, S., & Ahmad, K. (2014). Determining levels of urgency and anxiety during a natural disaster: Noise, affect, and news in social media. In *DIMPLE: disaster management and principled large-scale information extraction workshop programme*.

Krasnova, H., Veltri, N. F., Eling, N., & Buxmann, P. (2017). Why men and women continue to use social networking sites: The role of gender differences. *The Journal of Strategic Information Systems, 26*(4), 261–284.

Lee, H. J., & Stein, M. B. (2023). Update on treatments for anxiety-related disorders. *Current Opinion in Psychiatry, 36*(2), 140–145.

Lee, H. Y., Jamieson, J. P., Reis, H. T., Beevers, C. G., Josephs, R. A., Mullarkey, M. C., et al. (2020). Getting fewer "likes" than others on social media elicits emotional distress among victimized adolescents. *Child Development, 91*(6), 2141–2159.

Lin, Y. H., Lin, S. H., Yang, C. C., & Kuo, T. B. (2017). Psychopathology of everyday life in the 21st century: Smartphone addiction. In *Internet addiction* (pp. 339–358). Springer.

Mackson, S. B., Brochu, P. M., & Schneider, B. A. (2019). Instagram: Friend or foe? The application's association with psychological well-being. *New Media & Society, 21*(10), 2160–2182.

Madell, D. E. (2006). *Associations between social anxiety disorders and the social aspects of young people's internet and mobile phone use* (Doctoral dissertation). Durham University.

Mullin, A. C. (2017). *# comparison: An examination of social comparison orientation on Instagram as it relates to self-esteem and state anxiety* (Batchelor's dissertation). Claremont University.

Murdock, G. (2010). Shifting anxieties, altered media: Risk communication in networked times. *Catalan Journal of Communication & Cultural Studies, 2*(2), 159–176.

Nieminen, H. (2016). Digital divide and beyond: What do we know of information and communications technology's long-term social effects? Some uncomfortable questions. *European Journal of Communication, 31*(1), 19–32.

Niedenthal, P. M., Barsalou, L. W., Winkielman, P., Krauth-Gruber, S., & Ric, F. (2005). Embodiment in attitudes, social perception, and emotion. *Personality and Social Psychology Review, 9*(3), 184–211.

Pierce, T. (2009). Social anxiety and technology: Face-to-face communication versus technological communication among teens. *Computers in Human Behavior, 25*(6), 1367–1372.

Price, J. S. (2013). An evolutionary perspective on anxiety and anxiety disorders. *New Insights Into Anxiety Disorders, 3*, 20.

Rajaobelina, L., Prom Tep, S., Arcand, M., & Ricard, L. (2021). Creepiness: Its antecedents and impact on loyalty when interacting with a chatbot. *Psychology & Marketing, 38*(12), 2339–2356.

Reich, S., Schneider, F. M., & Zwillich, B. (2023). No likes–no control? Examining the role of coping deprivation and social anxiety in social media ostracism. *Behaviour & Information Technology, 43*, 1–14.

Rosa, H. (Ed.). (2010). *High-speed society: Social acceleration, power, and modernity*. Penn State Press.

Rosa, H. (2013). *Social acceleration: A new theory of modernity*. Columbia University Press.

Rosa, H., Dörre, K., & Lessenich, S. (2017). Appropriation, activation and acceleration: The escalatory logics of capitalist modernity and the crises of dynamic stabilization. *Theory, Culture & Society, 34*(1), 53–73.

Rosen, L. D., Whaling, K., Rab, S., Carrier, L. M., & Cheever, N. A. (2013). Is Facebook creating "iDisorders"? The link between clinical symptoms of psychiatric disorders and technology use, attitudes and anxiety. *Computers in Human Behavior, 29*(3), 1243–1254.

Scheff, T. J. (2005). Looking-glass self: Goffman as symbolic interactionist. *Symbolic Interaction, 28*(2), 147–166.

Seekis, V., & Kennedy, R. (2023). The impact of# beauty and# self-compassion Tiktok videos on young women's appearance shame and anxiety, self-compassion, mood, and comparison processes. *Body Image, 45*, 117–125.

Shabahang, R., Aruguete, M. S., & Shim, H. (2021). Online news addiction: Future anxiety, fear of missing out on news, and interpersonal trust contribute to excessive online news consumption. *Online Journal of Communication and Media Technologies, 11*(2), e202105.

Smail, D. (2018a). *Illusion and reality: The meaning of anxiety*. Routledge.

Smail, D. (2018b). *How to survive without psychotherapy*. Routledge.

Suarez-Villa, L. (2012). *Technocapitalism: A critical perspective on technological innovation and corporatism*. Temple University Press.

Suarez-Villa, L. (2013). *Globalization and technocapitalism: The political economy of corporate power and technological domination*. Ashgate Publishing Ltd.

Tams, S., Legoux, R., & Léger, P. M. (2018). Smartphone withdrawal creates stress: A moderated mediation model of nomophobia, social threat, and phone withdrawal context. *Computers in Human Behavior, 81*, 1–9.

Tanaka, M., & Chen, C. (2023). Towards a mechanistic understanding of depression, anxiety, and their comorbidity: Perspectives from cognitive neuroscience. *Frontiers in Behavioral Neuroscience, 17*.

Van Den Eijnden, R., Doornwaard, S., & Ter Bogt, T. (2017). OP-117: Are smartphone dependence symptoms related to FOMO, craving and withdrawal symptoms during smartphone abstinence? Findings from a natural experiment. *Journal of Behavioral Addictions, 6*(S1), 56–57.

Vander Dussen, A. (2021). *Photo posting on Instagram: A measurement of social comparison, social anxiety, and experiences of loneliness on Instagram* (Doctoral dissertation). The Chicago School of Professional Psychology.

Wilkinson, I. (2002). *Anxiety in a 'risk' society*. Routledge.

Zhao, N., & Zhou, G. (2020). Social media use and mental health during the COVID-19 pandemic: Moderator role of disaster stressor and mediator role of negative affect. *Applied Psychology: Health and Well-Being, 12*(4), 1019–1038.

CHAPTER 4

Modernity Has Failed: The Beau Idéal Has Been Disconnected

He had another cup of coffee, another cake, gulping them down, still looking at the clock every few minutes feeling a need to rush, no thought from what or to where, but only a vague yet crushing pressure of time, time that seemed to wrap itself around him like a python.
Hubert Selby Jr. (1964, Last Exit to Brooklyn)
Ma hypothesis is fucked. They'd rather gie a merchant school old boy with severe brain damage a job in nuclear engineering than gie a schemie wi a Ph.D. a post as a cleaner in an abattoir.
Irvine Welsh (1993, Trainspotting)

Abstract This chapter examines the symbolic exhaustion of modernity's promises: progress, futurity, social mobility. These narratives no longer hold meaning, sustained only by hollow gestures of connectivity and digital performativity. Drawing from Beck, Fisher, Suarez-Villa, and others, it argues that modernity no longer believes its own myths. The future merely replays the present with minor aesthetic updates. This recursive stagnation produces a culture of dread and anhedonia, where progress persists only as *spectacle*: an empty performance concealing the underlying, systemic collapse of cohesion and shared beliefs.

Keywords Modernity · Exhaustion · Alienation · Disconnection

N. N. Adams, *Terminal Destruction*,
https://doi.org/10.1007/978-3-032-22274-9_4

Revisiting Mark Fisher's work on capitalist realism, these notions present salient ideas for interrogating technological-mediated anxiety in *immediate modernity*. Fisher employs 'capitalist realism' to refer to notions that capitalist principles underpinning the architecture of Western economy, politics, personal sensemaking and social interactions are ever-present, impermeable, and operate in configurations propagating that there are no rational/viable alternatives to capitalist structuring (Fisher, 2022a). Fisher's work draws parallels with Gramsci's notions of cultural hegemony: an unquestionable and subversive societal ordering structure propagating a constrained guise of 'normalised reality' (Gramsci, 2011). However, Fisher differs from Gramsci's macro-hegemonic constraints by adopting a flexible, shifting macro-micro lens on social reality: at times, zooming out to discuss the capitalist structuring of politics, social policies and neoliberalist principles, then relocating perspectives more narrowly, linking ranging constructs to elucidate influences over mental health, workplace interactions, and micro-level social constructs (Fisher, 2022b).

Core to Fisher's concepts is the acknowledgement that capitalism does not necessarily represent the most desirable or positive structure for modernity. But the evolution of social systems—norms, rules and laws—centres capitalist principles in the fabric of their frameworks, so capitalism appears the only rational principle compatible with contemporary human nature. In contrast to Gramsci's subversive notions of political and social hegemony, Fisher frames capitalist realism as a *hypervisible* construct (i.e. highly visible and recognisable), permeating every interaction in society. Thus, overt success and subscription to capitalist principles in most forms of social interactions are the result of the promotion: the growing acknowledgement and complicacy to the idea that modern human desires are *only* compatible with capitalism. Alternative social structuring principles that are heterodox to personal accumulations of capital are perceived as incompatible with human nature. So: the ability of alternative systems to rise to governing structures for social interactions, transactions and ordering is made impossible by this manufactured hegemony that quells any arising dissonance (Fisher, 2022a).

A key example here is Fisher's reading of the 2007–2008 bank bailouts. These occurred because the collapse of the banking system was politically and socially unthinkable. Given the banks' practical and symbolic centrality to capitalism, their failure was never a viable option, despite immense financial losses. Rather than confronting the system's unsustainability, governments opted to place these institutions on 'life support'.

Fisher argues this move reinforced and legitimised capitalist realism, entrenching its hegemony while normalising the devaluation of workers and eroding the collective power of labour (Fisher, 2022a).

4.1 Capitalist Realism, Dopamine, and Technology

Theorising through this lens is useful when recontextualised to collective anxieties, particularly with regards to anxiety and sociotechnical accelerations. Adopting a Gramscian perspective on Fisher's thinking: the banking bailouts evidence less a *hypervisible* framing of capitalist realism in action, as it does a subversive interlaying of capitalist principles within social transactions. While the 'spectacle' displayed in the 2007–2008 financial crisis was the supposed peril of the capitalist banking system, similar capitalist-led structures operating as more *immediate* micro-social structuring constructs were unaffected, and in fact were centred and enjoyed capital growth at an otherwise defined point of financial collapse. For example, the first iPhone was released in mid-2007, becoming widely available in 2008 at a cost of $599 (equivalent of approximately $1168 in late-2025). The iPhone sold over 11 million units in 2008. That year, sales of Apple products were highlighted as experiencing growth sales of nine percent, Apple experiencing a single-quarter revenue record in the last three months of 2008. Similarly, quarter four 2008 Apple iPhone sales statistics record iPhone sales revenue at $806 million (Apple, 2008), at a time of recognised global financial precarity.

Following these logics, some constructs, like banking institutions, appear to be immune from *decline*—aka capitalist meltdown. The argument that follows should be read at two levels. First, as a sociological diagnosis of how capitalist and technological systems mutually reinforce each other through everyday use and cultural normalisation. Second, as a critical reading of the political and affective implications of this entanglement. In other words, while the analysis foregrounds the anxious and commodifying dimensions of digital capitalism, these are not presented as universally negative; rather, they exemplify how technological architectures distribute both constraint and possibility within the same circuits.

Certain technologies remain protected, even paradoxically profiting during periods of global uncertainty that might otherwise threaten capitalist dominance. This resilience stems from two interlinked factors. First, echoing the logic of the banking bailouts, capitalist hegemony sustains the notion that the only escape from capitalism is to *spend our way out*. Media narratives repeatedly reproduce this idea, promoting heightened transactional activity during crises to generate 'necessary' public economic confidence (Singh & LaBrosse, 2011). Second, technological capitalism succeeds because technological systems inherently propagate capitalist ideals and transactions, naturalised through their function as facilitators of social interaction. These propagations occur both overtly and subversively. Purchasing a technology item is an overt act of capitalist symbolism: the fulfilment of a commercial desire translating an invisible transaction into the visible ownership and operation of a technological object. The financial exchange remains largely obscured, occurring as 'closed' commerce between consumer and corporation, yet when used publicly, the object's visibility converts financial capital into social and cultural capital through the recognition/kudos attached to technological possession. Networked to this, technologies reinforce capitalism by simplifying and embedding cumulative capital-interactions as a secondary but pervasive function. A striking example within *immediate modernity* is Apple's App Store. Although the iPhone was marketed primarily as a mobile telephone, it instantly connected users to commercial platforms for music, gaming, and lifestyle products, encouraging constant consumption. In the UK, Amazon's shopping app launched for iPhone during the 2008 holiday season, coinciding with the peak of the global financial crash. These virtual shopping constructs, highly successful, transformed the iPhone from a communication tool into a portable gateway to continuous commerce: pleasures available at one's fingertips, anytime, anywhere. The device's celebrated status thus lies less in its communicative capacity than in its role as a conduit between human capitalist desire and the mechanisms of capitalist fulfilment, rendering it near indispensable.

In *immediate modernity*, social media has also become deeply embedded in everyday interactions, reshaping norms, behaviours, and social capital. Most platforms are now designed primarily for mobile devices, further cementing these as indispensable tools and portable status symbols. These technologies do not simply host capitalism, they *enact* it, embedding capitalist ideals within the rhythms of 'natural' social interaction. This reshaping of subjectivity extends beyond the social and symbolic into the affective and neurobiological textures of everyday life. Digital platforms do not sit atop technocapitalist systems, they are engineered to interface directly with the body's reward circuitry and their logics are biochemical as much as economic. Dopamine, often reduced in popular discourse to a crude 'pleasure chemical', is better understood as signalling anticipation, salience, and motivational pull: the neurological marking of what must be noticed, returned to, or repeated. Under *immediate modernity*, platform architectures have learned to exploit this system with extraordinary precision. Contemporary interfaces—notifications, infinite scroll, algorithmic curation, variable reinforcement—are built to trigger intermittent dopaminergic spikes. This is not incidental; it reflects the political economy of engagement, where every micro-interaction constitutes 'value'. Refreshing a feed, opening an alert, receiving a 'like': these actions become tightly timed reward cues that loop the dividual back into the system as predictable, exploitable patterns of behaviour. Having already decomposed the subject into fragments of affect, data, and gesture, these platforms then modulate those fragments through neurochemical hooks, with the system learning desire at the level of micro-prediction, identifying which cues extract the greatest return and recalibrating the environment to maximise repetition. What emerges is a behavioural economy that feels self-directed but functions as a soft, habituated compulsion. This dynamic exceeds the narrow framing of 'addiction'. It constitutes a patterned dependency produced by the material infrastructures of technocapitalism: an environment in which baseline reward thresholds are raised by constant micro-stimulation. As these stimuli accumulate, the salience of offline life is diluted, and embodied interactions begin to feel comparatively muted, lacking the rapid contingencies and instant affirmations that digitally-mediated exchanges reliably deliver. This contrast intensifies the gravitational pull of the technological bubble: actors gravitate towards the spaces that deliver the highest ratio of reward to effort, reinforcing a behavioural homeostasis that favours the digital domain. Crucially, this is not a private neurochemical effect but a structural one. Platforms leverage dopaminergic modulation to produce behavioural predictability at scale. Ease, connection, and efficiency are fused with intermittent reward in ways that normalise technologised existence as the default mode of being. In this sense, dopamine becomes another invisible protective layer for technocapitalism: a biochemical tether binding desire, repetition, and attention to the circuits that extract value from social actors.

In parallel, these dopaminergic hooks bind anxiety ever more tightly to the everyday textures of technologised existence. The very mechanisms that draw actors back into digital systems also sharpen the psychic turbulence of being there: the fracturing of self into curated fragments, the algorithmic cycling of crisis imagery, and the steady normalisation of low-grade distress. Anxiety becomes not an aberration but an ambient condition: an affective background that technological life both produces and depends upon. Crucially, the absence of technology is no relief from this pressure. As outlined earlier, disconnection carries its own destabilising charge: the sense of falling out of sync, missing something important, or drifting beyond the social horizon. This dynamic reveals communication technologies as a *catch-33*: their presence generates unease through comparison, crisis-exposure, and dividualised self-presentation, yet their absence generates a different, equally potent unease rooted in dislocation, loss of continuity, and perceptual detachment. The result is a recursive affective loop with no meaningful point of exit. Engagement produces tension, disengagement produces tension, and actors oscillate between the two in search of equilibrium that never arrives. This is not 'addiction' in the narrow clinical sense, but represents a structurally cultivated dependency: an affective circuitry within which anxiety becomes a rational, predictable outcome of systems designed to keep subjects attuned, available, and endlessly returning.

If dopamine functions as the biochemical tether that keeps actors circulating within technocapitalist infrastructures, everyday economic interactions reveal the parallel structural trap: a system where exploitations are visible, routinely recognised, yet largely met with weary resignation. Nowhere is this clearer than in the choreography of pricing algorithms and dynamic markets that structure contemporary consumption. Considering the purchase of concert tickets: what was once a straightforward transaction is now an event in itself. Actors are funnelled into digital waiting rooms, confronted with 'dynamic pricing', and forced to compete with automated purchasing systems that inflate scarcity. Prices spike in real-time, sometimes doubling or tripling within minutes, producing an acute, manufactured panic: *buy now or lose the experience forever*. The process is transparently extractive, yet deeply normalised. The user sees the exploitation unfold in front of them, understands it as such, and proceeds anyway. This is the quiet violence of technocapitalism: the system displays its mechanisms openly, and the actor accepts them because refusing feels impossible. The same dynamic unfolds in more mundane contexts. Train travel, for instance, increasingly operates through punitive pricing linked to disruption. A cancelled service does not stabilise fares for the next available journey; instead, prices surge the following day, as if the passenger's misfortune is an opportunity for natural capitalisation.

Airlines offer a similar example: cookies track search behaviour, noting the routes and dates one is considering. Each return visit to the same query becomes a signal of rising intent: a data point that justifies a price increase. The user is effectively punished for their own interest. Everyone knows this happens; advice to 'search in incognito mode' circulates as folk wisdom. Yet the structure persists, unchallenged, because it is baked into the accepted logics of the market. Similarly, movies on already-paid-for streaming services are now interrupted by tailored algorithmic adverts suggesting purchases, which can be 'added to your Amazon basket' at the click of a TV remote; podcasts pause to play sponsored adverts, overlaying discussions of mental health and wellbeing with catchy jingles directing listeners to private healthcare providers; and Google searches now display results in order of 'sponsored' services before the most relevant.

These patterns generate a distinctive affective atmosphere: a blend of irritation, low-grade anxiety, and a resigned sense that one must endure the whims of systems engineered to extract maximum value from minimal choice. The exploitation is banal, routine, and expected; within this hegemony lies power: technocapitalism positions the human actor as someone who must absorb these asymmetries, someone whose role is not to contest the system but to navigate it, tolerate it, and adapt to its shifting terms. Much like the dopaminergic hooks of platform design, these economic mechanisms train the actor to internalise the inevitability of exploitation. This hegemony renders structural manipulation indistinguishable from ordinary existence.

It would, however, be a simplification to frame these technological entanglements solely as instruments of domination. As Fisher noted in his later work (Fisher & Colquhoun, 2020), the digital sphere has also opened terrains for new collectivities, subcultural expression, and counter-hegemonic organisation. The same infrastructures that commodify attention can, under different conditions, facilitate resistance, community, and creative autonomy. For example, movements such as Occupy, Black Lives Matter, and Extinction Rebellion use corporate platforms to transform systems of visibility into tools of dissent and collective care. Open-source projects and encrypted networks likewise repurpose infrastructures of control into architectures of autonomy. Even within algorithmic cultures, users create spaces of refusal through glitch aesthetics, meme activism, or anonymous collectivity. These counter-hegemonic traces spotlight that technocapital's systems are never fully closed: capture and creativity coexist within the same architecture. Rather than propagate an unrealistic moral binary position between 'good/offline' and 'bad/online', the argument advanced here recognises that both tendencies coexist within technocapital's design. Importantly, *Acid Communism* reframed Fisher's earlier pessimism by seeking the latent energies of collective joy and solidarity within cultural life. Technology, for Fisher, could still harbour traces of this generative potential. While the analysis here acknowledges that optimism, it situates it within *immediate modernity*, where such counter-hegemonic spaces are fleeting and rapidly reabsorbed, but, of course, are still possible.

4.2 Theorising the Beau Idéal Disconnect

Immediate modernity is structured by a *hypertechnological*, realist, ever-present and pervasive form of normalised capitalism. While historically, societal structures are prone to reconfiguration per shifting social norms, disruptions, and changes in collective social sensemaking, capitalist structuring of social interactions is now constant and machinically self-replicating. As Fisher (2022a) argues, capitalism represents the primary embedded ordering structure for modern life; it is not allowed to fail. Thus, technocapitalism can be considered the cultural hegemony of *immediate modernity*.

Crombez (2021) explores the concept of anomie as a product of capitalist accelerations, with anomie defined as an uprooting and disintegration of structural values, linked to notions of social distancing, othering, and fragmented cohesions, and intertwined with the frame that capitalist late modernity paradoxically exudes euphoric tendencies. While Crombez discusses anxiety, and positions a simmering, collective dissonance, this does not manifest (or accelerate) into a full anxious disconnect. Similar positions are present in Suarez-Villa (2013) and Rosa (2013), exploring *Technocapitalism* (Suarez-Villa) and *Social Accelerationism* (Rosa), both contending with structural changes facilitating heightened interconnections between social actors, yet paradoxically, amplifying these connections to prioritise structures based on material wealth and production (Suarez-Villa, 2013). As Rosa puts it, these connections lead, ultimately, to a form of inertic "frenetic standstill" (Rosa, 2013, p. 71): humans struggling to comprehend or exist within a fractural stasis of constant accelerating change.

Drawing together the preceding chapters, *immediate modernity* reveals an inseparable coupling of technology and capitalism, each providing the other with invisible forms of protection. Their relationship is symbiotic, and at times dialectical: structuring reality in ways that make life inside the technocapitalist bubble smoother, easier, and often seductively pleasurable. Yet these conveniences remain narrowly circumscribed: technologies overwhelmingly reproduce capitalist logics, reinforcing rather than disrupting the hegemony that sustains them. Fisher's banking bailouts example illustrates this dynamic with clarity. The banking system's collapse represented a genuine heterodox moment, a point where capitalism could conceivably have failed. Instead, the crisis was rapidly contained and redirected into a rescue operation. The system was saved because it is structurally designed to save itself: materially, politically, and psychologically. Capitalism cannot be permitted to fail, and the technologies nested within it are configured to reproduce precisely this sense of inevitability.

The impermeable strengthening of the link between **technology** and **capitalism** in *immediate modernity*, the intrinsic protections afforded, and the pervasiveness of technological interactions as a necessity to interact with modern life may be conceptualised as a solid intersect of these two social structuring objects. Linked **technology-capitalism (T-C)**, while both positive and negative, is portrayed almost universally as a natural, rational, and positive interconnection resplendent of the *beau idéal* of contemporary living. Synthesising a clarified turn on this by reapplying Beck's (2009) theorising regarding *unintended risk* as a framing lens: these negative occurrences, often resulting in anxieties, are likely unintended and unforeseen consequences arising from T-C's hegemony.

Considering the above, *immediate modernity*'s anxiety pandemic may be understood as linked to the indelible rise of T-C. Principally, this can be explored as three interconnected points of occurrence that can be encompassed by the theory of *the beau idéal disconnect*.

Firstly, as demonstrated in the works discussed above, technology and capitalism are inextricably linked in *immediate modernity*. If capitalism functions as an inescapable macro-structuring principle, then the anxieties emerging from rapid sociotechnical acceleration are equally unavoidable. Though experienced at the micro-social level, these anxieties are woven into the fabric of capitalist hegemony-as-normality. Following Gramsci's notion of cultural hegemony, this interconnection is largely invisible—accepted as normal by most social actors. Contrary to scholarship that positions these structures as *hypervisible* (Crombez,

2021; Suarez-Villa, 2013), applying Gramscian thought to T-C illuminates its paradoxical strength: its invisibility. Rather than acting in overt hegemonic support of capitalism, social actors uphold consent through routine and complicit participation, reinforcing the norms that define social reality. Fisher (2022a) identifies any deviation from this order as unthinkable, casting dissenters as othered or deviant for rejecting capitalist logic. Thus, capitalist hegemony persists as a rational and necessary ordering construct—*the only reality compatible with human and social existence*—sold to actors as the *beau idéal* of *immediate modernity*. While commerce-of-convenience offers fleeting rewards of dopamine, social capital, and belonging, it paradoxically sustains a cycle of unfulfilled desire. Capitalist hegemony, therefore, endures through collective complicit consent, chaining actors to both its pleasures and anxieties.

Secondly, a novel disconnect arises when social actors recognise that the *beau idéal* of T-C produces not only pleasure but persistent anxiety. This realisation destabilises belief in T-C as a universally positive construct. Yet, as Fisher (2022a) notes, no visible alternative exists: opting out is impossible. So: even awareness of its negative consequences does not grant escape, since technological engagement is essential for functioning in *immediate modernity*. The resulting recognition: that actors are permanently tethered to technology and its anxieties, can be deeply disquieting, revealing the (largely) closed loop of a capitalist-technological hegemony from which withdrawal is unthinkable/impossible.

Thirdly, this disconnection solidifies when actors accept their situation as both unchangeable and accelerating. Reapplying Beck's (2009) theorising, actors come to see the risks of T–C as underplayed and its benefits overstated. For Fisher (2022a, 2022b), capitalist systems that have reached a certain apex of acceleration appear immutable. Following Land (2012), the only response to their momentum is further acceleration. In contrast to Crombez (2021) and Suarez-Villa (2013), this forward motion represents an uncertain self-perpetuation of T–C, sanctioned by collective hegemonic consent. As Beck (2009) observes, social actors thus face escalating uncertainty, compelled to move forward into a future whose risks remain opaque. Thus, capitalist culture reframes this anxiety as naturalised: an inevitable feature of progress, while the haunting spectre of *technology-to-come* looms as both promise and threat. This duality: progress entwined with obsolescence, captures the uncanny tension of *immediate modernity*, a culture suspended between dissonant acceleration and collapse. It is here that *the beau idéal disconnect* crystallises as a central source of collective, anxious uncertainty.

4.3 Summary

Chapters 2, 3, and this chapter establish *immediate modernity* as the defining structure of the contemporary moment, introducing *the beau idéal disconnect* as the mechanism through which collective anxiety is produced and normalised. This reframes anomie, restriction, and frenetic inertia as a single reactive formation, positioning anxiety not as deviation but as a structural feature of the present. Approaching technology, capital, and affect through this analytic lens clarifies how accelerating systems generate and sustain this collective condition. Chapters 3 and this chapter develop this further by mapping the recursive ties between technological acceleration and hegemonic capital. They argue that social actors are now bound to infrastructures of immediacy whose continual renewal collapses novelty and obsolescence into the same temporal field. *Immediate modernity* thus names a paradoxical state of simultaneous progression and decay: one that offers efficiency and pleasure while exposing individuals to systems that reproduce risk as a permanent atmosphere. *The beau idéal disconnect* captures this contradiction: the recognition that the very architectures enabling participation also manufacture chronic insecurity while foreclosing meaningful alternatives. Together, these concepts provide the theoretical ground for understanding the triadic entanglement of technology, capital, and collective affect. Chapters 5 and 6 extend this trajectory by interrogating *immediate modernity*'s anxious momentum through the lens of accelerationism.

References

Apple Inc. (2008). *Unaudited summary data*. https://www.apple.com/newsroom/pdfs/q408data_sum.pdf.

Beck, U. (2009). *World at risk*. Polity.

Crombez, J. M. (2021). *Anxiety, modern society, and the critical method: Toward a theory and practice of critical socioanalysis* (Vol. 182). Brill.

Fisher, M. (2022a). *Capitalist realism: Is there no alternative?* John Hunt Publishing.

Fisher, M. (2022b). *Ghosts of my life: Writings on depression, hauntology and lost futures*. John Hunt Publishing.
Fisher, M., & Colquhoun, M. (2020). *Acid communism*. Pattern Books.
Gramsci, A. (2011). *Prison Notebooks, Volumes 1–3*. Columbia University Press.
Land, N. (2012). *Fanged Noumena: Collected writings 1987–2007*. Urbanomic.
Rosa, H. (2013). *Social acceleration: A new theory of modernity*. Columbia University Press.
Singh, D., & LaBrosse, J. R. (2011). Developing a framework for effective financial crisis management. *Financial Market Trends, 2*, 26.
Suarez-Villa, L. (2013). *Globalization and technocapitalism: The political economy of corporate power and technological domination*. Ashgate Publishing Ltd.

CHAPTER 5

Deconstructing Accelerationism in Immediate Modernity

Abstract This chapter dismantles accelerationism's foundational wager: that speeding up capitalism might hasten its end. Rereading Deleuze and Guattari, Land, Fisher, and Xenofeminist-linked critiques, it argues that acceleration has long since been captured: repurposed, as the invisible engine of capital's persistence. Left and right variants of /Acc both misread the nature of movement, assuming speed/evolution still implies change. Thus, acceleration has become explanatory, not insurgent. This chapter clears conceptual ground for i/Acc: a new mode of analysis that decodes systems from within, rather than outpacing them.

Keywords Accelerationism · Ideology failure · i/Acc · *Immediate modernity*

To begin this chapter, I first acknowledge that diverse notions of accelerationism (/Acc) are already applied and invoked in existing scholarships. Recent commentaries within the broader accelerationist discourse have reflected critically on the theoretical inflation and popular misreadings of

---

The very forces of matter, in their blind advance, impose their own limits.
Albert Camus (1951, The Rebel)

N. N. Adams, *Terminal Destruction*,
https://doi.org/10.1007/978-3-032-22274-9_5

the term. Among the most incisive is Mattie Colquhoun's *Xenogothic* critique, which tracks how 'accelerationism' detached from its leftist genealogy to become an aesthetic or political provocation in itself.[1] Colquhoun situates this drift within a wider exhaustion of theoretical nuance in online culture, where accelerationism risks serving as a cipher for transgression rather than a framework for systemic critique. Engaging such internal critiques clarifies that the present account positions itself in conversation with this history: acknowledging the plural and sometimes contradictory life of /Acc thought while resisting its simplification into slogan or style.

Relatedly, /Acc scholarship can trend towards cherry-picking isolated 'accelerationist' examples: the speed of technology, the intensification of reactionary ideologies, or ecological degradation, while conflating accelerationism with mere intensification. Such reduction obscures the underlying drivers of action, prevents synthesis, and (often) miscasts L/Acc as inherently reactionary. In reality, /Acc origins and conceptual context lie firmly on the political left, offering a lens not of condemnation but of critical understanding and potential intervention. Srnicek and Williams in *Inventing the Future* (2015) reject the notion that accelerationism entails the uncritical celebration of technological speed or capitalist dynamism. Their project reframes acceleration as a strategy of repurposing: redeploying capitalism's productive and technological capacities towards post-capitalist ends. Earlier online discussions, archived fragments from *The Accelerationist Reader* (Mackay & Avanessian, 2014), *Plan C*,[2] and the early blogosphere, show a similarly experimental moment: accelerationism functioning as a space of political speculation rather than ideological alignment. Together, these sources demonstrate that L/Acc's emancipatory horizon lies not in intensifying capitalism for its own sake, but in strategically redirecting its mechanisms towards collective autonomy and social equity.[3]

[1] At the time of writing, Colquhoun's online writings could be accessed at: https://xenogothic.com/category/accelerationism/.

[2] At the time of writing Plan C could be accessed at: https://www.weareplanc.org/2014/03/accelerate-this-leeds-plan-c-discusses-the-accelerationist-manifesto/.

[3] Blog-based primary materials are cited only where reliably archived. Because such sources are inherently unstable—subject to deletion, editing, or loss—they are treated as evidence of discourse formation rather than as academic authorities.

Throughout this chapter, the term *acceleration* is used not to describe literal velocity or an enthusiasm for technological speed, but to denote the amplification of capitalism's internal dynamics and contradictions. Early formulations of accelerationism did not simply advocate 'speeding up' capitalism; rather, they sought to expose how capital's own mechanisms of intensification might produce points of exhaustion or transformation. The aim, therefore, is not haste but analysis: tracing the processes by which capitalism reproduces itself through perpetual motion and examining where those movements might generate rupture.[4]

Academic focus on developing accelerationist applications as a theoretical framework for understanding contemporary macro-level Western society—aka *immediate modernity*—is limited. To achieve this: Chapters 5 and 6 clarify, detangle and explore components of Left Accelerationism (L/Acc): firstly, collating perspectives from transdisciplinary thinkers, clarifying these into a coherent explanation of L/Acc; secondly, L/Acc is distinguished from disparate and arising contemporary /Acc variants; thirdly, historical 'accelerationist' theories and perspectives are reinterpreted, reconstructed and explicated; fourthly, these chapters draw together reinterpretations by clarifying theory, arguing that despite radical divides between accelerationist motives and desired outcomes: yes, as others posit, we are now ALL accelerationists. This conclusion is reached when considering processes of near-universal hegemonic and complicit support for technocapital subscription and intensification in the context of *immediate modernity*. Following this, L/Acc positions are transmuted, strengthening these as investigatory and explanatory constructs for application to wider social investigations. Implications for forward theorising and applications are presented in Chapter 6, and the new collective scholarly field of Investigatory Accelerationism (i/Acc) is introduced to 'reboot' transdisciplinary and radically collaborative accelerationist scholarship: promoting egalitarian social goals, within and outside the academy.

[4] "Acceleration" is employed here as a conceptual register rather than a kinetic metaphor: an index of systemic amplification rather than of physical pace.

5.1 Accelerationism—We're Just Getting Started

'Accelerationism' is frequently invoked in academic discourse, yet its meanings are dispersed and often contradictory. /Acc has been interpreted in ways that often diverge from its original theoretical concerns. A common misunderstanding, typically associated with 'right-accelerationist' rhetoric, frames left accelerationism as a call to push capitalism's destructive logic to its limits to provoke collapse. Fisher, however, argued that L/Acc is better understood as seeking to accelerate until reform or transformation becomes possible, rather than simply advocating systemic destruction. At the same time, it is worth acknowledging that readings emphasising 'acceleration-to-collapse and then subsequent rebuilding/repurposing' are not without legitimacy; much of the literature can be interpreted through this lens. Accelerationism has also been linked to provocative political manoeuvres, exemplified by Slavoj Žižek's suggestion that supporting a disruptive political figure could destabilise entrenched structures and reinvigorate leftist politics. As Richard Coyne notes, such approaches aim to 'shock' the system rather than articulate a coherent programme for change (Coyne, 2017). In this book, /Acc is not treated as a prescription for destruction or political theatre. Instead, it is employed as a lens for diagnosing the effects of *immediate modernity*: the intensification of social, technological, and economic flows that renders both possibility and crisis immediate. Thus, accelerationism is approached here as a structural condition, traced to illuminate how hyper-connected, high-speed systems configure experience, perception, and contemporary subjectivity. Reading /Acc this way highlights how capital relentlessly deterritorialises and reterritorialises social, psychic, and technological processes, transforming crises into momentum. The goal is diagnostic rather than prescriptive: to trace these dynamics, identify moments where they destabilise capital's logic, and consider how such excesses might be repurposed towards egalitarian ends. This methodological stance operationalises a new L/Acc-linked position: Investigatory Accelerationism.

As foregrounded by Chapters 2–4, *immediate modernity* denotes a triangular nexus: (1) pervasive, technology-mediated capitalist structures; (2) rapid technological and communicative accelerations, normalised by human actors as tools of cohesion yet reinforcing dopaminergic-mediated commodity fetishism; and (3) a diffuse, systemically produced anxiety, framed as a natural by-product of successful, productive engagement with technology and capital.

The claim that we are all accelerationists was previously argued by Shaviro: "accelerationism in philosophy or political economy offers us, at best, an exacerbated awareness of how we are trapped" (Shaviro, 2013, para. 16). The following sections advance this perspective, arguing that by being aware of the primary separate-but-interlinked mechanisms of societal accelerationist integrations that permeate *immediate modernity*, we can identify and pinpoint new structural components that drive this 'trapping'. The notion of technological hegemony is merged with Connell's identity interpretations of Gramsci's cultural hegemony, and linkages to Deleuze and Guattari's foundational notions of deterritorialised flow: an elemental accelerationist principle. This is to clarify the relations between technology, hegemony, and capitalism in *immediate modernity*—framing these interconnections against core L/Acc theory. This reorients /Acc with a focus on wider application and understanding, situated against a backdrop of society's unconditional complicit support at three levels of society. By demystifying accelerationism, and in particular the subfield of L/Acc, I argue that in Western, technology-medicated, capitalist society, social actors are routed to lend undeniable, complicit support to a pseudo-autocratic technological hegemony.

Collective 'accelerationist' consent is manufactured through polarised positions, yet the extent of this is often underestimated. The framework outlined here spotlights two dominant stances. First, capital structures are maintained to justify accelerating technological progress as essential for human survival, with cultural hegemony positioning capitalism as the necessary vehicle for this goal. Second, an opposing radical view sees acceleration as a form of heterodoxic disruption: destabilising the capitalist nexus, but as Shaviro (2013) argues, such actions may ultimately reinforce rather than subvert capital's logics. Both positions thus legitimise and reproduce the technology-capitalism (T-C) standard. A third, resistant stance does exist that suggests people can 'escape' from capital-led enclosures, but I argue that in *immediate modernity* participation in technocapitalist systems is functionally compulsory to avoid marginalisation. From a structural perspective, then, we are all accelerationists now.

5.2 L/Acc: Decoding Left Accelerationism and Distinguishing L/Acc from R/Acc

L/Acc can be interpreted along two sharply diverging axes. First: accelerationism as the intensification of capitalist processes themselves, aligning with Nick Land's de/reconstruction of the macro-capital nexus and the deliberate speeding up of capital's dynamics to reimagine—or 'accelerate'—society[5] (Land, 2012a, 2012b, 2017a, 2017b). While this trajectory is often read as Landian, it still sits within the orbit of L/Acc when understood through Fisher's lens. For Fisher, pushing capitalist processes to their limits can expose the cracks and contradictions that capitalist realism works so hard to suppress (Fisher, 2022a). Acceleration here is not an endorsement of capital per se but a means of forcing its presumed inevitability into 'crisis'. Via this framing, even accelerations routed through capital's own machinery retain L/Acc potential: they reveal the system's brittleness and open conceptual space for alternatives that capitalism insists are impossible. Second: L/Acc as a "modernity project" (Srnicek & Williams, 2015, p. 1177), one that seeks to selectively amplify accelerations within chosen sociotechnological domains while dampening them in others, with the aim of constructing a post-capital alternative grounded in equity. This position draws from, but has also in part been critiqued by Srnicek and Williams as the 'techno-fix paradigm' (2015). Here acceleration becomes a tool for redesigning, rather than reproducing, the sociotechnical order.

The contemporary L/Acc position takes shape through a lineage that runs from Deleuze and Guattari's provocation to accelerate capitalism's deterritorialising tendencies, through the Ccru's speculative technocultural experimentation, and into Fisher's reworking of accelerationist thought as a political-affective critique of capitalist realism (Fisher, 2022a). Fisher's intervention is crucial here: by foregrounding the psychic

[5] Land's relationship with accelerationism is complex. His work within and beyond the Cybernetic Culture Research Unit (Ccru) established key accelerationist principles influenced by Bataille (Land, 2012a), Deleuze and Guattari (1972, 1982), Lyotard (2015), Nietzsche, and Heidegger. Heidegger's notion that technology is never morally neutral but directed towards an inherent telos (Heidegger, 1977) is particularly evident in Land's writing. Land integrates this with Deleuze and Guattari's ideas, privileging *Anti-Oedipus* (1972) over *A Thousand Plateaus* (1982), to suggest that capitalist intensification should not be resisted but accelerated. This reframing sidelines concerns over the voids of inequality and collapse that such acceleration may produce.

and structural constraints that bind subjects to the present, Fisher renders visible the fractures through which alternative futures might be forced. Fisher's work traces both the promise and pathology of accelerated thought. His early examinations of *the flatline*, and its recurring dead/undead symbolism, situate acceleration as a psychic motif of suspended vitality: life extended yet hollowed, a metaphor for late-capitalist subjectivity. His later development of capitalist realism extends this inquiry, framing capitalism as an ontological enclosure where technological dependency and economic logic intertwine, producing a self-sustaining cycle of affective and cognitive capture (Fisher, 1999, 2018, 2022a). Across these works, acceleration functions as both mechanism and symptom: the generative engine of capital and the processes through which conditions of alternative possibility are consumed. Srnicek and Williams (Williams & Srnicek, 2014; Srnicek & Williams, 2015) draw threads together into a systematic L/Acc programme. Reading their formulation: technology is not inherently capitalist, yet neither does technological development automatically yield progress. They argue that technology must be deliberately redirected rather than rejected or left to market logics. The techno-fix paradigm proposes that specific accelerations: automation, infrastructure, platforms, computational capacity, can be intensified and repurposed to build post-work futures, redistribute power, and expand collective capacities. This position addresses a long-standing political impasse in which the left critiques capitalism's technological formations but offers no alternative technological horizon. Through this framing, acceleration becomes less a surrender to capital; it is redirected as a strategic effort to reclaim the future by actively shaping the direction of technoscientific development.

Thus, at its conceptual centre, L/Acc seeks not the abolition of capitalism but its redirection. Through processes of overload, reinterpretation, and repurposing, L/Acc positions theorise a strategic reconfiguration of capital's internal dynamics. Read through a Gramscian lens, this can be understood as a project of hegemonic reversal; revealing how technological and economic structures sustain dominance not through repression, but through the manufacture of consent and the normalisation of capitalist rationality. As such, L/Acc reframes capitalist hegemony as a power susceptible to intellectual revolution: a détournement of the cultural mechanisms that bind social actors to systems of exploitation, and the reclaiming of agency through conscious acceleration. This reading positions accelerationism as both diagnostic and emancipatory. It recognises capitalism's productive capacities but demands their selective amplification and reorientation towards collective good. In this, the L/Acc project advances tightly moderated accelerations within technocapital: capital emergent from and sustained by technology, rather than wholesale intensification. The objective is systemic recalibration, not implosion. Core to this proposition are the arguments for Universal Basic Income (UBI) and the full automation of labour. By decoupling survival from employment and transferring productive functions to automated systems, exploitation becomes structurally redundant. Production can then accelerate without human cost, dismantling entrenched hierarchies and allowing social organisation to reconfigure around equity, autonomy, and collective utility (Fisher, 2022a, 2022b; Fisher & Colquhoun, 2020; Srnicek & Williams, 2015). In this sense, L/Acc forms an insurgent optimism: an attempt to weaponise acceleration as a route towards reorganisation, liberation, and post-capitalist possibility.

5.3 Distinguishing R/Acc

Given recent Western media fixation on R/Acc, and its visible adoption by far-right and supremacist networks, it becomes necessary to restate the distinction between L/Acc and R/Acc as ideologically divergent rather than interchangeable extremes. Much public discourse collapses these trajectories into a single, reactionary current, framing accelerationism as a monolith of technological nihilism. This reductionism obscures the critical utility of /Acc thought, folding a complex genealogy of ideas into a moral panic about speed, automation, and collapse. Once framed solely through the lens of extremism, accelerationism becomes ideologically toxic: its theoretical potential erased by proximity to its most corrupted form. Yet this erasure is deeply ironic as early articulations of accelerationism were not projects of collapse but of reconfiguration, representing efforts to rethink capitalism's machinery from within its own dynamics of mutation. To dismiss accelerationism because of its neoreactionary distortion is to abandon a lens capable of exposing precisely the systems that have weaponised it. Theoretical tools, like technologies, are never fixed in meaning; they circulate, are repurposed, and can be reclaimed. Beauchamp (2019) notes this tension, distinguishing L/Acc's emancipatory trajectory from R/Acc's regressive turn, one seeking collective liberation through transformation, the other fetishising collapse as destiny. As Haynes (2021) argues, R/Acc represents a distinctly neoreactionary orientation that "embraces the project of capitalism" (p. 1177), amplifying its exclusionary logics in the pursuit of selective destruction and authoritarian renewal. This strand of thought remains closely tethered to Nick Land, whose later writings—allegedly—provide its conceptual architecture. For Land, capital operates as an accelerating feedback loop: an autopoietic system of compression, intensification, and recursive expansion. In *immediate modernity*, this loop becomes visible in the seamless fusion of algorithmic cognition and global commerce: the neural mesh of finance and AI. From the algorithmic routines of WhatsApp to the predictive architectures of high-frequency trading, cognition and capital now move as one continuous current: reading Land, acceleration is not failure, it is fulfilment. Capital does not implode under the weight of its own velocity, it evolves through it (Land, 2012b). As such, creative destruction becomes the grammar of endurance, a mechanism by which capital sustains its hegemony through perpetual mutation. Technological proliferation, in this sense, is not the symptom of capitalism's *decline* but its guarantee: an endless recursion that folds collapse back into continuity.

Via this lens, L/Acc frames as heterodoxic to R/Acc's nihilism, as a deliberate, tempered practice: acceleration as strategy as opposed to a spectacle. Where R/Acc exploits speed to magnify inequality and destabilise, L/Acc seeks to channel the same forces towards reconfiguration, repurposing capital, and technology to expose structural hierarchies and redistribute agency. It is a project of controlled amplification: selective theoretical acceleration aimed at revealing the underlying logics of domination while preserving the possibility of radical intervention. In reclaiming the discourse from misappropriation, L/Acc restores accelerationism to its original, left-critical purpose: a lens for diagnosing, understanding, and ultimately transforming the entwined structures of technology, capital, and social power in *immediate modernity*.

Beyond theory, the R/Acc perspective has been linked to notions of 'crisis accelerations', with these positioned to destabilise governments via both violent and socially disruptive means (Michael, 2005). R/Acc has also been interpreted as justifying the rejection of democracy: upholding governmental corruptions as proof of democracy's fundamental failure (Beauchamp, 2019). Elaborating, Burrows (2018a, 2018b) presents a deconstruction of R/Acc, including a networking of trajectory between R/Acc and Land's neoreactionary perspective—itself linked to the wider NRx movement (neoreactionaryism). While a detailed deconstruction of NRx is beyond the scope of this book (and would represent a multi-chapter work), broadly, NRx refers to a clarified—hyperised—R/Acc perspective also termed *The Dark Enlightenment* (Land, 2012b). Land[6] reframes freedom as fundamentally incompatible with democracy, rejecting egalitarianism in favour of a post-libertarian, technologically mediated authoritarianism. *The Dark Enlightenment* envisages the obsolescence of modern nation-states, replacing them with centralised regulatory architectures designed to optimise efficiency and governance. Democracy, via this frame, is not a neutral mechanism but a structural hindrance to progress, slowing the velocity of capital and decision-making. Media commentary frequently conflates NRx with the alt-right, presenting it as a theoretical arm of contemporary reactionary politics. Yet, critical scholarship clarifies the distinction: Noys (2014) indicates that NRx positions an acceleration of capitalism to a fascist point, while Land himself disavows direct links to fascism, noting that fascism operates as a mass, anti-capital movement, whereas NRx seeks to intensify, extend, and accelerate capital's reach. Jones (2019) further situates NRx within the intellectual currents of postmodern critique and affect theory, highlighting its analytical engagement with modernity's failures, yet distinguishes it from broader alt-right discourse through its deliberate synthesis of historical, philosophical, and theoretical registers. Thus, NRx cannot be read simply as a populist movement, but a speculative, accelerationist experiment in governance and social order: a thought architecture testing the limits of capital, technology, and hierarchy, deliberately decoupled from egalitarian or democratic norms. In this sense, *The Dark Enlightenment* functions as a conceptual extremity of *immediate modernity*: an exploration of what happens when the imperatives of capital and technology are pushed towards maximal acceleration, unconstrained by conventional social or political ethics.

In summary, R/Acc stands in contrast to L/Acc, lacking the relational and selective frameworks that enable constructive application. It prioritises pro-capitalist ideologies while driving acceleration towards destructive outcomes.

[6] I acknowledge here that Land's writings vis-à-vis *The Dark Enlightenment* are heavily influenced by the writings/theorising of Curtis Yarvin.

5.4 Amalgamate-Manifold Alternate /Acc Formations: Decoding 'Effective' and 'Unconditional' Accelerationist 'Form' and 'Anti-Praxis'

Recently, some notions of accelerationism have arisen that amplify, reject, and blur distinctions between L/Acc and R/Acc ideologies and practices. Academic scholarship on these notions is sparse; instead, ideological discussions and concepts commonly play out in various online spaces.

Effective Accelerationism (E/Acc) has emerged as a notable strand within contemporary /Acc discourse. E/Acc builds on some of Land's foundational theorising, particularly regarding the inextricable link between capital and AI (Land, 2017a, 2017b). E/Acc positions unrestricted technological progression—driven by AI acceleration—as the principal mechanism for addressing humanity's most pressing existential crises: climate change, resource scarcity, and global conflict. In this respect, E/Acc aligns with the emancipatory potential envisaged by L/Acc. However, E/Acc departs from the selective, critically mediated acceleration championed by L/Acc. Where L/Acc emphasises deliberation in deciding *what* to accelerate, E/Acc rejects such selectivity, framing preferencing as a brake on systemic progress. This philosophy legitimises accelerating AI development to the threshold of artificial general intelligence, echoing Land's conception of the technosingularity: a radical reconfiguration of society and cognition that is presumed universally beneficial. Yet, in practice, the movement rarely engages with the attendant risks of delegating complex societal decision-making to autonomous systems. Within technological development organisations, E/Acc is often described as a form of 'effective altruism' or 'techno-optimism' (Soufi, 2024), but this optimism is grounded in faith regarding AI as a solution, rather than critical assessment of its likely unintended consequences (thus ignoring Beck's *risk-society-reflexive-modernity* positions outlined in Chapters 2 and 3). As such, the E/Acc position conforms to Srnicek and Williams' (2015) L/Acc critique of technological naivety: the argument that an overreliance on technology as a solution to modernity's capitalist-mediated constraints is unlikely to originate from a 'ramping up' of technological acceleration alone.

Unconditional Accelerationism (U/Acc) presents a markedly different, more enigmatic strand. Emerging predominantly within online spaces, U/Acc defines itself through rejection: it claims ideological neutrality, eschews political alignment, and self-identifies as 'anti-praxis'. That is, U/Acc resists structured theorising, institutional frameworks, and normative mediation, favouring decentralised, striated flows of acceleration. This extreme anti-praxis, however, renders formal theoretical engagement with U/Acc problematic. Any attempt to summarise or systematise its principles risks violating its self-declared essence. Consequently, U/Acc is acknowledged here primarily as a conceptual presence: a fringe, fluid, and fragmentary construct within the broader accelerationist landscape, rather than a coherent theoretical model amenable to analysis or application.

Other forms of accelerationism have developed to focus on specifics components of society, identity, and existence. Importantly, Xenofeminism and Gender Accelerationism (G/Acc) are different ideological movements both encapsulating frames of resistance and new freedoms within identity-genders/non-gender arenas.[7] Xenofeminism engages directly with contemporary feminist thought, seeking to reconfigure and expand the emancipatory potentials of gender politics through the lens of technological/bioscience acceleration. It foregrounds the accelerating pace of scientific and digital technologies, exploring how these tools might be harnessed to dismantle existing hierarchies and reimagine structures of gendered power. Therefore, Xenofeminism operates as a form of applied accelerationism: deliberately deploying the dynamics of technological intensification towards social transformation. Gender Accelerationism, by contrast, pushes this logic further, treating gender itself as a site for maximal acceleration. G/Acc contends with the expansion and destabilisation of gender norms to the point of systemic and conceptual collapse, emphasising disruption as a mode of critique and potential liberation. Both Xenofeminism and G/Acc, while differing in scope and strategy, are rooted in accelerationist thought, drawing on the principle that intensifying the forces of technology, social practice, and structural critique can open new emancipatory possibilities. A full deconstruction of these movements lies beyond the scope of this work, yet their inclusion illustrates how accelerationist frameworks extend beyond economic and technological domains, permeating social, cultural, and identity-based arenas. They demonstrate the breadth of /Acc thought: not merely a critique of capital or technocapital, but a conceptual tool for exploring radical reconfigurations across multiple axes of contemporary life.

[7] For an overview of Xenofeminism see Cuboniks (2018). For an overview of Gender Accelerationism see Storm and Flores (2020).

5.5 A 'de' and 're' Construction of Core Accelerationist Concepts and Historical Theorising: A Rereading of Accelerationism and its Contradictions

The following sections function as an **interpretive rereading** of existing psychoanalytic and post-psychoanalytic theory, revisiting established frameworks through the lens of *immediate modernity*. As outlined in Chapter 2, this work draws from psychoanalytic vocabularies to interrogate the production of desire and subjectivity within the accelerating structures of the *immediate* present. Here, it becomes necessary to clarify how and why these vocabularies are mobilised. The discussion that follows does not seek to reconcile traditions, but to use them diagnostically: to treat Lacanian psychoanalysis and Deleuze–Guattari's schizoanalysis as conceptual instruments, each illuminating different aspects of the same systemic condition. Lacanian psychoanalysis operates through language; desire emerges through the Symbolic order, structured by law, signifier, and the intersubjective codes that organise subjectivity. The Oedipal complex functions as the formative knot: binding the subject to the law of the Other and inaugurating lack as the constitutive condition of being. In contrast, Deleuze and Guattari dismantle the notion of lack, reframing desire as productive flow: a machinic process of connection, decoding, and recombination. Schizoanalysis reads the unconscious not as theatre but as factory: a site of continuous assembly, capture, and escape. In *immediate modernity*, both lenses remain vital. A Lacanian reading helps expose the linguistic and ideological architectures through which subjects internalise capitalist realism, while a schizoanalytic approach traces how technocapitalist systems generate and redirect desire through networks, platforms, and machinic assemblages. The two overlap in their diagnostic potential but diverge in orientation, with one reading subjectivity through its structuring absences, the other through its proliferating excesses. To maintain precision, this chapter explicitly signals which register is being deployed at any given point. References to the Real, the Symbolic, the Imaginary, or the desire of the Other indicate a Lacanian framing; references to desiring-machines, deterritorialisation or the unconscious as productive circuitry signal a schizoanalytic one. This transparency matters, as the argument that follows depends on using these frameworks less as fixed doctrines but as tools for reading how desire, language, and machinery intersect under *immediate modernity*'s accelerating conditions.

Deleuze and Guattari's neomaterialist[8] work *Anti-Oedipus* applies de/reterritorialisation constructs to human psychology. Analysis here employs a schizoanalytic frame, foregrounding desire as productive flow rather than structural lack. This is necessary for grasping how technocapital channels and accelerates subjectivity in ***immediate modernity***. Deleuze and Guattari argue Freud's thinking vis-à-vis the human psyche—introduction of structuring applications evidencing the conscious and unconscious, drives and polymorphous developmental dichotomies (Freud, 1929)—led to a revolution in conceptualisations vis-à-vis understandings of human thoughts, perceptions, intentions, and actions. Established notions of the human psyche were ***deterritorialised***: established thought regarding functioning and mechanisms, operating parameters and influence was made visible, deconstructed, and rationalised. The established mechanisms by which humans understood psychology were brought under challenge, yielding new perspectives of consideration. To react to this challenge, Freud's notions of the Oedipus complex formed a process of ***reterritorialisation*** in the same space: creating new conceptualisations and (re)constructions, with Freud developing novel understandings of the psyche incorporating functional notions of repression underpinning *desire*, intentions, and actions: a subsequent ***reterritorialisation*** of notions regarding the human psyche (Deleuze & Guattari, 1972).

Rereading processes via a psychological lens, the above paradigm links with Piaget's assimilation and accommodation notions regarding rational thought operating as a developmental-sensemaking strategy of ordering: for accepting the evolving complexities of social reality and interactions (Piaget, 1968). However, unlike Piaget's notions of reactive schema questioning: the updating and re-appraising of reality when so-called ineffable truths are challenged, Deleuze and Guattari range this psychological reterritorialisation away from the individual and the micro, applying the same broad theoretical principles of challenge-and-update to macro-collectivist society and networks of human actors' formulations of understanding for the social realities they inhabit. This draws parallels with Gramsci's notions of hegemony—Gramsci extrapolating a theory of collective social consent towards a seemingly natural macro-level political structuring order from notions of individual consent and challenge (Gramsci, 2011).

[8] The exploration of meaning in a material world defined by commodities, inspired by Marxist and Engelian thinking, see Lefebvre (2009).

Rereading *Anti-Oedipus*: Deleuze and Guattari apply the above theorising to capitalism. They increase the ***ranging*** of social deterritorialisation when considering capitalism via a macro-social contextual lens. Deleuze and Guattari can be read to argue capitalism—and associated hegemonic capital imperatives and desires—encompasses a massive collection of ongoing deterritorialised flows. Decoding this: capitalist impulses, structuring and interactions, hallmarks of Western existence, represent configurations of continually updating, modifying, and accelerating processes of trend development and portrayal, rejection, and reiteration: networked threads of hegemony. Interpreting this at its most raw, functional level in modernity, this structural propagation leads to a hegemonic cultural imperative of progressive object-seeking, spending and commodity fetishism, with capital operating as an anchoring structure that continually updates human wants and needs in line with shifting trends, ensuring ***desire*** is constantly evolving; never stagnating. Again, reinterpreting Deleuze and Guattari: this represents a rejection of the personal unconscious desires popularised by Freud, with actors now oriented instead to develop drives to represent a factory construct: a mechanic production of specific ***socialised desires*** (i.e. following a learned pattern of hegemony coded per Piaget's assimilation and accommodation framework). However, this forward, reactive movement still lends to framing per Freudian terms, linking to the collective ***libidinal drive*** theory of Western society developed by Lyotard (Lyotard, 2015). Importantly, Lyotard's work on Libidinal Economy divorces from some of the (post)structural[9] Marxist notions invoked by Deleuze and Guattari (1972). Here the argument returns to a Lacanian–Lyotardian register, using drive and jouissance to reveal how technocapital engineers intensities and excitations as core mechanisms of ***immediate modernity***. Lyotard acknowledged the limitations of 1970s critical theory and (post)structural Marxism, divorcing from viewing society as anchored primarily by a systemic constellation of ***desires***, and instead, adopting a semiotics-led approach that reconceptualises (indeed, at least partially reterritorialised)

[9] I have chosen to include the qualifier "(post)structural" to describe Marxist interpretations developed in Deleuze & Guattari's *Anti-Oedipus*. This is because the authors' relationships with Marxism is complex and does not represent a stable or clear trajectory of interpretation that defines notions, even where this is presented in clarified terms: see Deleuze (1953). Others have also recognised this position.

Freud's *drive* to network with Lacan's notions of *Jouissance*: the regulation and transgression of individual and collective pleasures and linked drives and motivations (Lacan, 1988, 2011; Lacan et al., 1993). Thus, following the above theoretical journey, societal drives operate as a structuring principle, with *libido*—complex, shifting desire and regulation—flowing through networked drives to realise social occurrences, form, and action, with Lyotard ultimately being read here as this process validating capitalist structuring as both natural and pleasurable both in its positives and 'perverse' negatives.

Situating this against the context of *immediate modernity*, we may consider capital to be the dictating force *regulating* drives, or: Deleuze and Guattari's *flow*. The interpretive scale now widens from the intrapsychic to the systemic: psychoanalytic concepts are redeployed at the collective level via Gramsci, clarifying how desire is organised through cultural-technological hegemony. Structuring and libidinal regulation claims can be qualified and interpreted via rereadings of Gramsci's foundational notions of cultural hegemony (Gramsci, 2011). Hegemony represents a repressive social control structure dominating society not via repressive bodily punishments and conflicts, but instead through networks of ideological control, belief-management, and propagation (Gramsci, 2011). Speaking to this perspective, Deleuze and Guattari (1982) among other scholars (e.g. Giddens, 2007; Tomlinson, 2003) reify the concept of mediatisation: influence of mass media technologies on controlling constructs of (de/re)territorialisation and linked capital-desire. Scholars centre media constructs as fundamental, connecting human actors towards specific capitalist wants, operating as a catalyst for triggering individualistic enterprise-drives and competitive desires. For example, constructing and maintaining divides between specific fashions, technology brands and labels. In tandem, media constructs propagate, and maintain capital investments via upholding of the competitive paradigm as normality: hegemony representing a natural product of material existence in modernity and an instinctive[10] and unquestioned expression of libidinal drive, defined by Freud as the central motivator behind human behaviour, an emotion of existence—a psychical drive (Trieb) that connects bodily excitation with representation and object-seeking (Freud, 2015).

Synthesising these perspectives: I reinterpret Deleuze and Guattari's notions of de/reterritorialisation via overlapped lenses of Lyotard, Gramsci and Piaget, as a constant flux of shifting capitalist desires communicated to society's populace via technological mediatisation: an interlinked nexus of pro-capital flow and drives. This achieves a shifting yet permeable blueprint of 'competitive capital normality' imparted on the population as hegemony: encouraging ongoing assimilating and accommodating of wants and needs, with *desires* shifting with enough frequency as to keep the populace restless and desiring more purchasing power, commercial goods, and commodities as a means to fulfil capitalist engagements, but normatively not restless enough to question the existing capitalist status quo or to attempt to displace ingrained technological mechanisms of hegemony via the stoking of a revolutionary rejection of capitalist normality. This process at its nexus represents the *structure* of competitivity and continued object-seeking: the *libidinal drive* towards continued capital engagement and commodity fetishism, as opposed to the by-product function: a fulfilment of capital commodity itself. Thus, the above reinterpretation of *drive* as applied to capital negotiations in contemporary technological society may be considered the current capital hegemony of *immediate modernity*.

Crucially, some accelerationist theorising suggests disruptions to the existing capitalist hegemony via intermediary interventions that question the value of commodity fetishism and consumer culture are unlikely to

[10] The term *instinct* appears in early English translations of Freud's work (notably by James Strachey in the *Standard Edition*: see Freud & Strachey, 1964), where it was used interchangeably with *Trieb*. However, contemporary Freudian scholarship recognises that *Trieb* more accurately translates to *drive*, not *instinct*. The distinction is significant: *instinct* implies a biologically predetermined, automatic behaviour, whereas *drive* (Trieb) denotes a psychical force that is both somatic and representational, structured through language, culture, and desire. In the context of *immediate modernity*, this book adopts *drive* to highlight how libidinal energies are socially and technologically mediated rather than innately fixed. This nuance better situates the argument within a terrain where affective impulses are continuously redirected by technocapitalist systems, rather than emerging from any essential or 'natural' human core.

succeed. This is because these reactions run contrary to the culture of complicit and normative consent that capitalist mediatisation ingrains in society as a key structuring principle of hegemony. Thus, social actors are unlikely to take actions towards the dismantlement or 'repurposing' (following L/Acc) of capitalist principles, as this would equate to destabilising and dismantling the very fabric of the social reality within which they exist. Interpreting this through Piaget's notions of accommodation: this perspective represents a complete rewriting of the self, comparable to a psychological crisis of identity, which actors are unlikely to voluntarily instigate (Piaget, 1968). Some notions of L/Acc advocate for rapidly accelerating capitalist technological intensifications and associated commodity-related propagations of desires and wants, capitalist growth and infrastructure, to uncontrollable and unpredictable levels, signalling change. The hypothesised result is that, due to capitalism's inherent internal contradictions and instabilities, unchecked *accelerated* technological growth will disrupt structuring mechanisms: technology, mediatisation, commerce, and consumerism that represent the foundation for capitalist hegemony, leading to reconfigurations. This process is heralded as more likely to succeed, given that the trajectory of change—or *capitalist deterritorialisation*—occurs from acceleration and intensification of an existing and established trajectory, versus the requiring of a direct heterodoxic challenge to established hegemony.

Despite the attractiveness and oft-attached action-potential networked to the 'repurposing' L/Acc approach, when broken down, there are several fundamental issues when advocating such a position. Notably, some works critique accelerationism from the perspective that while anti-capitalist accelerations claim to be able to 'repurpose' structures of capitalism for essentially *hyper*capital-heterodoxic (anti-capitalist and egalitarian) means, the pathways and functions by which structures are repurposed and function in a post-capitalist reality are recurrently unclear (Gardiner, 2017; Shaviro, 2013, 2015). This is valid: the central consideration being that some L/Acc thinking hinges on a *supposition* that capital structures can both be repurposed *and* that a post-current-capital-reality will be inherently functional, equal, and positive, in the absence of evidence. Here, it is necessary to differentiate between voluntarist readings of accelerationism, which attribute transformative potential to sheer human will or political intensity, and the explicitly anti-voluntarist positions articulated within L/Acc itself. Srnicek and Williams, for instance, reject the idea that acceleration can be willed into being by subjective fervour or affective commitment. Their position is rigorously structural: capitalism is understood as a material system whose contradictions unfold independently of individual intention. Similarly, Williams' early writings on xenoeconomics conceptualise capital as a non-human process of abstraction and self-organisation, operating per logics that exceed agency. These currents reorient accelerationism away from voluntarist heroics towards an anti-anthropocentric analysis of the systems that condition human and post-human life alike.

To address core issues: firstly, and reinterpreting Deleuze and Guattari notions of deterritorialisation, should capitalist structuring be dismantled and made unusable via accelerationist means, deterritorialisation provides a theoretical framework to understand the instability and finality of this occurrence. However, despite the popularity of L/Acc notions of 'capitalist repurposing' claiming an accelerationist focus, this position lacks the reterritorialisation restructuring arm of sensemaking: how society can be (re)structured post-capitalism, and what structuring principles resemble. A further linked issue here is represented by the question of whether society can be conceptualised in post-capitalist terms from within the current, enclosed capitalist circuit of *immediate modernity*. To clarify: any projected hypothesis of a post-capitalist culture is capital-tethered: constructed irrevocably from within the current capitalist nexus, that operates as an immediate structuring principle for everyday life. The influence of this hegemony permeates **all** aspects of contemporary cultures, including academic scholarship and thought, as well as individual-collective micro–macro sensemaking. All existing objects within the capital nexus become subjugated, bound by capital logic. Thus, any hypothetical lens from which a future, possible post-capitalist perspective may be hypothesised is irreversibly tainted, and suppositions from this perspective must be treated as potential untruths: speculative fictions originating from a temporality nexus point different from the intended destination at which theorising will be applied. This raises the question to L/Acc:

> ***How can we suppose an alternative non-capitalist utopia from within an accelerating and all-pervasive capitalist hegemony?***

Relatedly, capital operates as the dominant structuring principle for Western society, an anchoring construct for desires and wants, which in turn constructs collective—hegemonic—libidinal drive towards generating means for commerce. If, following *drive* as the central force of existence, we concede drive-as-force is now inexorably interconnected with competitive and self-updating pursuits of capital, and this process is continually auto-reimagined to maintain hegemony, then it is immediately unclear what society (as human existence) will structurally represent following the dismantlement of the present capital quo. Fundamentally it is unknown if new arising structures may represent a positive or negative construct for the many, and how, or in what ways, new existence may disrupt established human drives propagated around navigating the capitalist-existence-structure of *immediate modernity*. Thus, and rechannelling Freud, Piaget, Lyotard and Gramsci:

> ***How will a sense of self be constructed in this new reality, and what may this look like, given the removal/repurposing of capital, a foundational identity-structuring construct?***

Linking, we may also ask:

> ***What libidinal drives will replace capitalist pursuits, and will replacement represent force(s) of equal or lesser destructive or positive potential?***

And:

> ***How—and in what ways—will any reconfigured drive operate as a functional structuring force for society, and how will integration of this drive(s) be negotiated, accepted, or rejected?***

Considering the L/Acc thesis that capitalist restructuring can be 'repurposed' with new schema for ordering social normality and mapping to alternative processes, the above perspective is equally—infinitely—challenging to conceptualise, given the unbalanced stance that much accelerationist theorising focuses almost exclusively on the *deteritorialising* of capitalism, with less emphasis on how dismantlement may be conducted in ways that appraise and protect structures supposedly capable of positive and functional repurposing, before these are *reterritorialised* into constructs for which no prior description or plan of function exists. This position is tantamount to readily trading a visibly priced commodity for an unknown, invisible, and intangible promise of a 'better deal', without information about transaction, costs, and potential losses. While some may contend any alternative to present quo is ***bound to be better***, this is a soft argument absent of functional evidence.

As a final point, L/Acc theory also appears often to discount or dismiss the potential human costs of accelerations. Manifold evidence exists supporting the position that humans get hurt via sociotechnological accelerations. For example, accelerations in social media use have many complex effects on human perceptions of wellbeing and self-worth (Sabik et al., 2020), accelerations in AI have been shown to construct deep anxieties for social actors linking to disruptions in what it means to be human and raising questions about the future of humanity, employment, and self-worth (Li & Huang, 2020) (see Chapter 4).

Considering arguments collectively, acceleration/repurposing of capital cannot be read as a strategy for liberation, but as an index of how crisis has been naturalised as the engine of continuity within ***immediate modernity***. The discussion here returns to a Lacanian logic of lack and contradiction, spotlighting why accelerationism reproduces the very instabilities it seeks to resolve within ***immediate modernity***'s recursive loops. To 'speed up' is not to transcend capital but to enact its logic more faithfully: accelerationism does not introduce instability so much as reveal how instability already functions as capital's sustaining rhythm. Crises are not external shocks to the system, they are the system's primary fuel, continuously produced, absorbed, and redeployed to preserve the appearance of movement. Thus, rather than endorsing the intensification of systems to a point of engineered fracture to facilitate repurposing, this chapter repositions crisis as the very mechanism through which technocapital reproduces itself. Any acceleration of existing trajectories amplifies human vulnerability within this recursive machinery: it heightens anxiety, precarity, and psychic fragmentation long before it could ever promise renewal. The wager of acceleration, therefore, is not salvation through speed/progress but confrontation with the truth that capital thrives on its own disorders. To recognise this position is not to advocate for further crisis but to expose the structural conditions that make crisis perpetual; and, crucially, to ask how those conditions might finally be interrupted rather than accelerated/repurposed.

5.6 *Technological Hegemony*: The Deterritorialised Flow Paradox

As positioned earlier in this chapter, *this* moment, *immediate modernity*, can be encapsulated by the rapid rise, parallel triangulated overlap, and interplay of three co-occurring cultural objects. The first of these is the enduring presence of a pervasive, transmutable, and hypernormalised[11] capital form linked to technology. This technological capital exists as cultural hegemony: unquestioned, an accepted and ruling construct, now impermeably structuring human lived existence. The second is the unparalleled, momentous, and shifting social advances connecting human actors ever more inexorably tethered to this capital framework, encapsulated by the necessity of operating, integrating, and increasingly relying upon technology as a product of simple *existence* and *survival* in *immediate modernity*. Together, these first two points can be considered as **the technological hegemony**. This links to multiple fragments describing technocapital and Land's specific notions of technocapital, yet also maintains divorce from some existing technocapital concepts.

Linking this back to observations within Chapter 4, each sub-domain of technocapital engages differently with the dialectic of deterritorialisation and reterritorialisation that structures *immediate modernity*. Platformic labour, for instance, deterritorialises the boundaries of work and leisure by dispersing production into everyday digital practices, yet reterritorialises this activity within the metrics of the platform economy, converting social interaction into measurable data. High-frequency trading deterritorialises human temporal experience, replacing the interval of decision with machine-speed transactions; reterritorialisation occurs as financial institutions integrate these automated logics into the normative architecture of markets. Pharmaceutical and biotech systems deterritorialise the body by transforming mood, cognition, and biological function into modifiable parameters, only to reterritorialise the self within regimes of biomedical governance and commercial dependence. These cycles of unbinding and recapture are not anomalies but represent the *constitutive rhythms* of technocapitalism. They spotlight how

[11] I use this term to refer to the normalisation of capitalism beyond simply hegemony: all pervasive to a point of total acceptance.

contemporary systems maintain both fluidity and control: dissolving traditional forms of mediation while establishing new infrastructures of regulation. The deterritorialising force of digital networks, financial automation, and biomedical intervention does not liberate the subject; instead these architectures produce a static-frantic condition of continuous reassembly, in which identity, labour, and affect are perpetually decomposed and recomposed per shifting logics of valuation. This dynamic gives rise to the ***dividualsubject***, a key conceptual figure within *immediate modernity*. The dividual emerges as the human correlate of technocapital's differential operations: a self fragmented across the various circuits through which it is made productive. On social platforms, the dividual is partitioned into data points and behavioural metrics; within financial infrastructures, it is abstracted into risk profiles and consumption patterns; within pharmaceutical and biotech systems, it is molecularised into chemical balances and genetic potentials. Each technocapital sub-domain therefore enacts its own mode of dividuation, operating on different scales, informational, economic, biological, to translate subjectivity into computable form. Understanding technocapital through these differentiated operations reframes deterritorialisation not as a singular theoretical occurrence but as a multi-scalar process whose effects are uneven and interdependent. It also highlights the central claim of *immediate modernity*: that contemporary subjectivity is constituted through its exposure to these overlapping regimes of technological and economic modulation. The human is not only located within technocapital but equally is dispersed through it, reproduced at the intersection of its multiple sub-domains. By distinguishing between pervasive technocapital and its specific operational strata, the analysis here retains fidelity to the material heterogeneity of the present. It also situates the ensuing discussion of affect, acceleration, and *decline* within the concrete infrastructures that sustain them, avoiding the abstraction of technocapital into a totalising entity, while maintaining its coherence as the systemic core condition of *immediate modernity*.

This layered understanding of technocapital returns us to the core dynamics of deterritorialisation and reterritorialisation. Each technocapital sub-domain operates as a site in which these forces intersect, producing variable configurations of stability, rupture, and recomposition across economic, social, and psychic registers. Rather than functioning sequentially, these processes now unfold simultaneously within the immediacy of technocapital's circuits. The deterritorialised subject of *immediate modernity* therefore inhabits a permanently transitional condition, one defined much less by simple displacement than by continual re-encoding within the overlapping architectures of finance, platformicity, and biopolitical mediation. As such, technocapital is utilised in the quasi L/Acc sense here: a questioning lens to identify the operational structures within technological hegemony. Unlike Land's self-reconfiguring technocapital, technological hegemony is not accelerating naturally towards a position of technosingularity, delocalising and banishing requirements for human involvement. Instead, it is accelerating towards a position of complete dominance and necessity in all aspects of human social functioning, to be indispensable: *indelible*, with all replicated structures of flow within the machine mirroring this necessity in their design. This position recognises Land's notions of technological hegemony as operating in complete control of capital markets (Land, 2012a), but also I argue that this position has now been largely achieved within *immediate modernity*; yet discordantly, this position is not immediately operating to rapidly usher in a post-human reality. This is primarily because humans represent the mechanic engine of *immediate modernity*: both the primary manufacturer and impetus, the purpose for manufacture of capital desire, resource, and propagation. So: the current operating paradigm is necessary, and by extension, *immediate modernity*'s accelerational feedback loop operates to temper accelerations that delocalise or reduce the role of humans in this system, to avoid an overload destroying the most salient purposeful power source within the structure: the human. As discussed at length in Chapter 3, *immediate modernity* also has a third object: all-pervasive, heightened and collectively-experienced anxiety, a disruptive and dysfunctional construct. This is positioned as a natural product of technology-capitalism presence, inexorable capital engagements, and ongoing accelerations: a de facto baseline for functional existence in contemporary reality for which anxiety-ownership and responsibility are delocalised to individuals, as opposed to anxiety acknowledged as a product of technology-capital or *T-C presence* and forced hegemony.

The ways in which this—overt and total *accelerationist*—technological hegemony maintains cultural dominance can be best interpreted by utilising Connell's identity framework adapted from Gramsci's original political hegemony theory (Connell, 2020; Gramsci, 2011). Connell argues that in modern Western society hegemonic masculinity (HM) operates as the most valued and policed form of masculine identity, one defined by strength, stoicism, emotional distance, independence, and dominance. This ideal is sustained through patriarchal dividends, normative conditioning, and a reward–punishment structure that discourages deviation. Connell identifies HM as functioning across local, regional, and global levels, producing a tiered system of masculine dominance. First, hegemonic masculinity proper refers to men who most closely align with and reproduce this ideal, gaining the greatest cultural legitimacy and structural advantage. Second, complicit masculinities uphold HM by not resisting it, supporting its dominance through everyday conformity. Third, marginalised masculinities sit outside or against HM; their practices neither support nor reinforce it, rendering them subordinated, othered, and positioned as incompatible with the hegemonic order (Connell, 2020).

Reinterpreting Connell's tiered framework and divorcing theory from masculinities, then attaching this to *immediate modernity*'s technological hegemony, we are left with three categories of social functioning: **hegemonic support, complicit support, active opposition**. From this vector, the accelerationist present becomes wholly restrictive, when considering how actors may invoke L/Acc theory as practice and de/reterritorialise capital circuits towards a co-opted liberatory future.

Firstly: social actors are routed—unconsciously—into the first two categories: direct and complicit support for technological hegemony. Justifying this: it is functionally impossible to operate in *immediate modernity* without interacting, relying upon and furthering technologies linking to the current capital quo. For example, bank accounts, medical records, simple commerce, smartphones and their services, communications, electronics, online shopping, physical shopping: all route individual social actors into this nexus. Operating within this nexus legitimises infrastructure demand—justifying quo requirements, yet withdrawal is functionally impossible. Thus, presence operates as a marker of hegemonic consent.

Secondly: the ubiquitous generation of human-data, data from all humans and their manifold interactions, is salient. Data collected is fed into multiplus electronic systems and networked to AI constructs. The means of ownership of this data have been delocalised: social actors must consent to the use of their data and relinquish data-ownership to use necessary technologies within the technological hegemony. To withhold consent restricts necessary access, shifting active and complicit consent into oppositional and marginalised territories. Thus, the actor is disavowed social technologies and necessary capital-technology engagements, which attach to everything. Resultantly, consent is given by actors as a means of functional permission, allowing actors to operate within technological hegemony (i.e. to *live*), and both legitimising and facilitating the capitalising of their involvement as data, which is then utilised to accelerate capital agendas and legitimatise hegemonic structuring.

Thirdly, complicit positions describe actors who may reject technological hegemony and attempt to limit how much of their data or behaviour is captured, their engagement in commerce, and online praxis. Yet because technocapitalist processes permeate all aspects of social life, withdrawal is impossible; at best, involvement can be reduced. Actors' consent thus becomes systemised: an automated outcome of structural necessity rather than active agreement. This is how control operates within *immediate modernity*'s technological hegemony: participation becomes essential.

Fourthly: those who actively oppose *immediate modernity*'s technological hegemony are few. Most opposition is token. Actors may actively discuss the concept of opposition, but this is rarely functionally realised. This is because these same individuals are left paradoxically operating in direct or complicit technological hegemonic support, while ideologically promoting an ideal of opposition, due to active opposition being near-impossible. This is the engineered perfection of *immediate modernity*, where posting on a blog, printing a manifesto, publishing a manuscript, all constitute a contribution of fragments as useful digital *data* that actively furthers an AI-mediated technological hegemony. Therefore, even resistance becomes support; generating data as contributory capital to further strengthen the hegemonic nexus. Those who attempt to resist technology (and therefore capital itself) as a means of conjuring resistance are marginalised. Marginalisation occurs via social ostracisms conjured directly by withdrawing integration privileges to social aspects of the technological hegemony nexus. For instance, withdrawing from social media removes individuals from connections to other actors. Relinquishing a smartphone (and all linked digital applications) negates direct contact with the many for whom this is a primary tool of connection. Refusal to own a debit or credit card narrowly restricts commerce, cash becoming ever more seldom used, carrying knock-on effects over credit score and ability to secure lending, purchase a property, a car, and increasingly secure employment. These factors all functionally restrict ability to exercise tangible resistance.

References

Beauchamp, Z. (2019). *Accelerationism: The obscure idea inspiring white supremacist killers around the world*. Vox. https://www.vox.com/the-highlight/2019/11/11/20882005/accelerationism-white-supremacy-christchurch

Burrows, R. (2018a). Urban futures and the dark enlightenment. In *Philosophy and the city: Interdisciplinary and transcultural perspectives* (pp. 245–258).

Burrows, R. (2018b). *On Neoreaction*. The Sociological Review. https://thesociologicalreview.org/collections/undisciplining/on-neoreaction/

Connell, R. W. (2020). *Masculinities*. Routledge.

Coyne, R. (2017). *What's wrong with accelerationism—Reflections on Technology, Media & Culture*. https://richardcoyne.com/2017/05/14/whats-wrong-with-accelerationism/

Cuboniks, L. (2018). *The xenofeminist manifesto: A politics for alienation*. Verso Books.

Deleuze, G. (1953). How do we recognize structuralism? *Desert islands and other texts, 1974*, 170–192.

Deleuze, G., & Guattari, F. (1972). *Anti-Oedipus: Capitalism and schizophrenia*. University of Minnesota Press.

Deleuze, G., & Guattari, F. (1982). *A thousand plateaus: Capitalism and schizophrenia*. University of Minnesota Press.

Fisher, M. (1999). *Flatline constructs: Gothic materialism and cybernetic theory-fiction* (Doctoral dissertation). University of Warwick.

Fisher, M. (2018). *K-Punk: The collected and unpublished writings of Mark Fisher (2004–2016)*. Repeater.

Fisher, M. (2022a). *Capitalist realism: Is there no alternative?* John Hunt Publishing.

Fisher, M. (2022b). Ghosts of my life: Writings on depression, hauntology and lost futures. John Hunt Publishing.

Fisher, M., & Colquhoun, M. (2020). *Acid communism* (Vol. 13). Pattern Books.

Freud, S. (1929). The economic problem of masochism. *The Psychoanalytic Review (1913–1957)*, *16*, 209.

Freud, S. (2015). Beyond the pleasure principle. *Psychoanalysis and History*, *17*(2), 151–204.

Freud, S., & Strachey, J. E. (1964). *The standard edition of the complete psychological works of Sigmund Freud*. Macmillan.

Gardiner, M. E. (2017). Critique of accelerationism. *Theory, Culture & Society*, *34*(1), 29–52.

Giddens, A. (2007). *The consequences of modernity*. 1990. Polity Press.

Gramsci, A. (2011). *Prison notebooks* (Vols. 1–3). Columbia University Press.

Haynes, P. (2021). Is there a future for accelerationism? *Journal of Organizational Change Management*, *34*(6), 1175–1187.

Heidegger, M. (1977). The question concerning technology. *New York, 214.*
Li, J., & Huang, J. S. (2020). Dimensions of artificial intelligence anxiety based on the integrated fear acquisition theory. *Technology in Society, 63*, 101410. https://doi.org/10.1016/j.techsoc.2020.101410
Jones, A. (2019). From neoreactionary theory to the alt-right. In *Critical theory and the humanities in the age of the alt-right* (pp. 101–120).
Lacan, J. (1988). *The seminar of Jacques Lacan: Book 1: Freud's papers on technique 1953–1954.* CUP Archive.
Lacan, J. (2011). *The seminar of Jacques Lacan: Book X: Anxiety: 1962–1963.*
Lacan, J., Miller, J. A. E., & Grigg, R. T. (1993). The seminar of Jacques Lacan, Book 3: The psychoses 1955–1956. In *Translation of the seminar that Lacan delivered to the Société Française de Psychoanalyse over the course of the academic year 1955–1956.* WW Norton & Company.
Land, N. (2012a). *Fanged Noumena: Collected writings 1987–2007.* Urbanomic.
Land, N. (2012b). *The dark enlightenment.* Imperium Press.
Land, N. (2017a). *A quick-and-dirty introduction to accelerationism.* Jacobite Magazine. https://web.archive.org/web/20180113012817/https://jacobitemag.com/2017/05/25/a-quick-and-dirty-introduction-to-accelerationism/
Land, N. (2017b). Nick Land Interview 2017. *YouTube* [Accelerate Baby]. https://www.youtube.com/watch?v=AGxgGQpyBYM
Lefebvre, H. (2009). *Dialectical materialism.* University of Minnesota Press.
Lyotard, J. F. (2015). *Libidinal economy.* Bloomsbury Publishing.
Mackay, R., & Avanessian, A. (Eds.). (2014). *# Accelerate: The accelerationist reader.* MIT Press.
Michael, G. (2005). The globalization. *Journal of Counterterrorism & Homeland Security International, 27*(4), 34.
Noys, B. (2014). *Malign velocities: Accelerationism and capitalism.* John Hunt Publishing.
Piaget, J. (1968). Le point de vue de Piaget. *International Journal of Psychology, 3*(4), 281–299.
Sabik, N. J., Falat, J., & Magagnos, J. (2020). When self-worth depends on social media feedback: Associations with psychological well-being. *Sex Roles, 82*, 411–421.
Shaviro, S. (2013). Accelerationist aesthetics: Necessary inefficiency in times of real subsumption. *E-Flux Journal* [online]. Issue 46. https://www.e-flux.com/journal/46/60070/accelerationist-aesthetics-necessary-inefficiency-in-times-of-real-subsumption/
Shaviro, S. (2015). *No speed limit: Three essays on accelerationism.* University of Minnesota Press.

Soufi, D. (2024). *"Accelerate or die": The controversial ideology that proposes the unlimited advance of artificial intelligence*. El País. https://english.elpais.com/technology/2024-01-06/accelerate-or-die-the-controversial-ideology-that-proposes-the-unlimited-advance-of-artificial-intelligence.html

Srnicek, N., & Williams, A. (2015). *Inventing the future: Postcapitalism and a world without work*. Verso Books.

Storm, V., & Flores, E. (2020). The gender accelerationist manifesto. *S. l, 24*.

Tomlinson, J. (2003). The agenda of globalization. *New Formations, 50*, 10–21.

Williams, A., & Srnicek, N. (2014). #Accelerate: Manifesto for an accelerationist politics. In R. Mackay & A. Avanessian (Eds.), *#Accelerate: The accelerationist reader* (pp. 347–362). Urbanomic.

CHAPTER 6

Identifying the Deterritorialised Flow Paradox of Immediate Modernity: Reconstructing Accelerationism as *Investigatory Accelerationism*

The future is not a straight line. It is filled with many crossroads.
There must be a future that we can choose for ourselves.
Kiyoko from Akira (1988, directed and written by
Katsuhiro Otomo and written by Izo Hashimoto)
Of course, the whole point of a Doomsday Machine is lost,
if you keep it a secret! Why didn't you tell the world, Eh!?
Dr. Strangelove from Dr Strangelove (1964, directed by Stanley Kubrick)

Abstract This chapter marks the theoretical pivot of this work. Building on Deleuze & Guattari's flow theory, and revisiting Land, Fisher, and later /Acc formulations, it identifies the paradox of *immediate modernity*: movement is constant, yet transformation absent. Capital's flows no longer *functionally* deterritorialise: they loop endlessly. Investigatory Accelerationism (i/Acc) is introduced as an alternative approach, using the logic of speed as a diagnostic tool rather than a weapon of rupture. i/Acc reads immediacy as data, repetition as code, and stagnation as revelation, turning the mechanisms of acceleration inward to expose their operations.

Keywords i/Acc · Deterritorialisation · Accelerationist methodology

N. N. Adams, *Terminal Destruction*,
https://doi.org/10.1007/978-3-032-22274-9_6

Applying the framework from Chapter 5 exploring tiered hegemony—revealing propagated, engineered participation and consent, *the deterritorialised flow paradox of immediate modernity* can now be identified and explored. *The deterritorialised flow* paradox refers to the automated removal of components of resistance that develop anti-technological hegemony or anti-capital sentiments, via a process of deterritorialisation linked to the context of changing flows and drives. This is represented by two differing theory possibilities explaining the failure of L/Acc processes in *immediate modernity*.

Firstly, and on one explanatory side, the 'invincible' structural reality argument can be posited:

> L/Acc-linked attempts to induce fail-states to redirect capitalism only end up feeding the wider technocapital machine (see arguments by Land, 2012, 2013, 2017). Read through Chapter 5's framing. This is unsurprising: what appears as targeted accelerations are often confabulations produced within a system whose hegemony shapes perception itself. Technological hegemony generates complicity, resistance, and indifference through the same ingrained processes, meaning actors inside the machine are structurally unable to determine which components could be meaningfully accelerated, repurposed, or muted (i.e. L/Acc's central thread). The system's interlocked flows appear simply as 'life as normal', rendering selective intervention impossible. This ultimately explains the stagnation of L/Acc's strategy of repurposed disruption.

On the other explanatory side, a related 'masochistic' reality-post-structural argument can be posited:

> This thread centres the position that *immediate modernity*'s technological hegemony constructs—inescapably—both positive and negative affect for human actors. Actors' maintenance in the prison of hegemony is developed, intensified, and permeated from the stance that actors partake in and are ordered by capital interactions: continually de and re territorialising capital *flows*, because these generate pleasure and desire, are structurally necessary for existence and survival, and because no functional process of resistance or restructuring is accessible.

Human actors are also harmed by this process in multiple ways. *Immediate modernity* binds the capital–technology–hegemony nexus to the production of anxiety, generating conditions in which psychic life is increasingly destabilised. Deconstructing this through Deleuze, Freud and Lyotard positions the following analysis primarily within a schizo-analytic frame: the rapid de/re-flow of experience becomes so accelerated that it interrupts Deleuze's notion of the fold: the process through which subjects take in the world, digest it, and project it outward as an identity-forming loop. Under *immediate modernity*, this loop is flattened into continual de/reterritorialisation, a condition that prevents the consolidation of stable meaning. As these pressures mount, the argument here necessarily shifts into a Lacanian register, where this persistent instability is read as a disturbance of the Symbolic order itself, producing a form of anxiety that reflects the difficulty of securing any coherent psychic foothold. Experience is projected before it is assimilated, resulting in cultural decay that is sustained only by capital's own drives. In this configuration, capital, through its technological hegemony, maintains the broader societal structure, diminishing human influence in favour of system-preservation. This is the lived condition of *immediate modernity*. This instability, returning to my earlier position from the close of Chapter 5, complicates any ability to distinguish (in the simplest terms) 'good' from 'bad' accelerationist threads. The construction of self-identity becomes entangled with anxiety, producing mixed affective states that resist simple categorisation. Although many elements of capital remain pleasurable, the current hegemonic nexus corrupts the pleasure principle, a moment best read through Lacanian jouissance (Lacan, 1988; Lacan et al., 1993), where pleasure and distress are routed through the same symbolic machinery.

Applying interpretations of Lyotard and Freud deepens this reading; here analysis moves into Freudian drive theory to clarify how pleasure emerges precisely through destabilisation. Lyotard identifies capital as pleasurable in both its constructive and 'perverse' forms, while Freud's work on masochism and Thanatos: the death drive, illuminates how capital overrides instinct, hollowing out the human self in favour of process. Under technological hegemony, pleasure is increasingly routed through anxiety: pain and tragedy. The disaster news economy exemplifies this dynamic: hyperreal media delivers devastation occurring elsewhere, allowing viewers to stabilise their sense of luck or safety. Tragedy becomes socially functional through its circulation, and virtual news infrastructures rely on these affective hooks to drive engagement. The addictive nature of disaster-scrolling arises not because harm is inherently pleasurable, but because tragedy is packaged and circulated as an affective commodity, producing desire, sustaining engagement and generating digital capital. This synthesis of Freudian drive and Lyotard's libidinal economy underpins one of the hardest recognitions within accelerationism under *immediate modernity*: pain becomes reliably transmuted into pleasure.

Taken together, structural hegemony and the corruption of pleasure severely limit the possibilities for L/Acc. Disagreement persists over what could be accelerated without reproducing harm. From a functional perspective, the answer may be 'nothing' if the goal is a genuinely egalitarian redistribution of capital, desire and flow. This captures the prevailing condition of accelerationism under *immediate modernity*: a technological hegemony operating as a self-transmuting structure of control and capital-generation, positioning humans as generators, conduits, and receivers of capital. In contrast to expectations that unrestrained acceleration ultimately forces a revolutionary rupture, the contemporary landscape resists this trajectory. Capital promotes only its own interests. Any 'creative destruction' resulting from acceleration would be interrupted by capital's regulatory mechanisms. Land's positive-feedback model remains highly relevant insofar as the ever-evolving capitalist system of *immediate modernity* self-prevents circuitry overload: velocity is kept high but never permitted to reach destructive thresholds. Capital therefore protects its own trajectory, continually adjusting its flows to maintain stability. At times this requires modulated de-acceleration—not slowing down, but holding velocity—to ensure hegemonic continuity. Revisiting the position that crises strengthen rather than collapse capitalism, I argue that selective L/Acc accelerations inevitably intensify, rather than disrupt, the power of technological hegemony. This intensification braces hegemonic imprinting rather than subverting via assemblage, undermining assumptions that L/Acc is inherently reformative. Under current conditions, it is impossible to determine what should be accelerated or to differentiate socially generative from socially destructive flows. With psychoanalytic and schizoanalytic registers working diagnostically throughout—tracking how desire, instability and machinery converge—the outcome is clear: stagnation becomes inevitable in *immediate modernity*.

6.1 Investigatory Accelerationism—i/Acc

Synthesised /Acc debates signpost that L/Acc can only progress by identifying which elements of capital should be accelerated to produce egalitarian change. Yet in *immediate modernity*, technological hegemony blurs resistance and amplifies every capital-supportive flow, rendering this task incoherent. L/Acc has therefore stalled, not only theoretically but structurally, because all actors now, willingly or not, participate in accelerating capital. The task is not to escape this condition but to clarify it, reorient the theory, and build a more realistic pathway forward.

Investigatory Accelerationism emerges from the recognition that traditional accelerationist projects have reached an impasse under the conditions of *immediate modernity*. Where Landian acceleration dissolves into capital's delirial self-intensification, and where L/Acc repeatedly stalls over the practical question of *what* should be accelerated and *how*, i/Acc begins from a different premise. i/Acc assumes that acceleration cannot meaningfully function as a strategy until we first understand the system that acceleration operates within. In other words, acceleration is not a tool to wield, but a phenomenon to read. i/Acc reframes speed, blockage, and repetition as diagnostic signals. Rather than treating acceleration as inherently emancipatory or inherently corrosive, i/Acc approaches it as data: evidence of how flows move, where they congeal, where they are captured, and how technological hegemony shapes the very perception of choice. Under this lens, stagnation does not indicate theoretical failure but reveals the system's architecture: its thresholds, its defensive mechanisms, its capacity to absorb and neutralise resistance. No existing /Acc thread has paused long enough to map these conditions; i/Acc makes this its starting point. Crucially, i/Acc acknowledges that in *immediate modernity* there is no exterior vantage point from which acceleration can be cleanly directed. All actors—complicit, resistant, ambivalent—are already folded into capital's circuits. Thus, any viable accelerationist theory must begin by making these entanglements visible. i/Acc foregrounds this visibility: it interrogates constraints, identifies how technological hegemony produces affective capture, and traces the recursive flows that generate both compliance and anxiety. Its purpose is not to abandon L/Acc but to rebuild the conditions under which L/Acc could function meaningfully. Where previous 'accelerationisms' approached the future as something to rupture into, i/Acc rejects this romanticism. It insists instead on orientation, granularity, and systemic realism. i/Acc tests, not assumes; it asks what happens when particular flows are intensified; what collapses, what strengthens, what mutates. It asks which accelerations can be safely deployed, which must be restrained, and which are illusions of agency generated by the system itself. Acceleration and deceleration become investigative tools rather than ideological commitments. In this sense, i/Acc performs a missing methodological step; it does not claim to resolve accelerationism's contradictions but to map them, clarify them, and create the theoretical space from which meaningful intervention might finally emerge: it is therefore not a new doctrine of disruption/reconfiguration but a disciplined reopening of the field: an approach that uses acceleration to study the system before ever attempting to transform it. The following section outlines a minimal conceptual framework for applying i/Acc theory as a diagnostic tool to the capital logics of *immediate modernity*.

6.2 i/Acc: A Minimal Applied Plan

1. Begin with exposure.

Map the hegemonic terrain as it is, not as theory imagines it. Identify the automated flows, silencers, feedback loops, frustrations, and points where agency collapses into system-preservation. Clarify the constraints before touching the accelerations.

2. Diagnose the stall.

Read repetition, stagnation, and apparent 'movement' as data. Treat loops, glitches, and stalled intensifications as signals revealing where capital's circuitry self-protects. i/Acc does not assume rupture is possible, its first task is to understand why it isn't.

3. Identify safe accelerants and necessary brakes.

Not all speed/evolution is emancipatory, and not all slowing/disruption is reactionary. I/Acc tests which processes generate harm when intensified, and which may open micro-spaces for equity, resilience or redistribution when modulated. This is experimental and always provisional.

4. Reassemble trajectories.

Develop altered flow-paths: small, realistic, material, rather than abstract utopias. I/Acc works through constrained re-routing: recalibrating systems so that acceleration serves human ends rather than subsuming them.

5. Iterate without purity.

i/Acc accepts complicity as a starting condition. It refines strategy through cycles of evaluation, feedback, and recalibration, recognising that every intervention carries cost. Progress emerges through sustained diagnostic engagement, not through fantasies of escape.

6.3 Summary

This chapter exposes the core paradox of *immediate modernity*: everything accelerates, yet nothing meaningfully changes. Capital's flows loop back into themselves, absorbing resistance, neutralising disruption, and converting pleasure, anxiety, and subjectivity into fuel for its own continuity. Under these conditions, L/Acc stalls; selective acceleration becomes impossible to aim, and every intervention is folded back into technocapital's circuitry. To progress, the chapter introduces Investigatory Accelerationism; i/Acc makes the system's constraints visible, interrogates where its flows stagnate or distort, and identifies how carefully modulated acceleration or restraint might open small but meaningful sites for social and egalitarian possibility. It offers a renewed trajectory for accelerationist thought, centring diagnostic clarity.

References

Lacan, J. (1988). *The seminar of Jacques Lacan: Book 1: Freud's papers on technique 1953–1954*. CUP Archive.

Lacan, J., Miller, J. A. E., & Grigg, R. T. (1993). The seminar of Jacques Lacan, book 3: The psychoses 1955–1956. In *Translation of the seminar that Lacan delivered to the Société Française de psychoanalyse over the course of the academic year 1955–1956*. W. W. Norton.

Land, N. (2012). *Fanged Noumena: Collected writings 1987–2007*. Urbanomic.

Land, N. (2013). Teleoplexy: Notes on acceleration. In R. Mackay & A. Avanessian (Eds.), *#accelerate: The accelerationist reader* (pp. 509–533). Urbanomic.

Land, N. (2017). A quick-and-dirty introduction to accelerationism. *Jacobite Magazine*. https://web.archive.org/web/20180113012817/https://jacobitemag.com/2017/05/25/a-quick-and-dirty-introduction-to-accelerationism/

CHAPTER 7

Hyperstition: A Primer

Abstract This chapter interrogates hyperstition: the process by which fictions become real through their circulation. Drawing on Land, Ccru materials, and Fisher, it explores how symbols, memes, and narratives accumulate force as they loop through affective and algorithmic systems. Hyperstition is not interpreted as speculative fantasy, but as infrastructure: mechanics through which belief itself generates material effects. This primer outlines how recursive symbolic processes shape both the social imagination and the perceived limits of 'the real' within *immediate modernity*.

Keyword Hyperstition · Nick Land · Symbolic systems

During the 1990s, English philosopher Nick Land and the Cybernetic Culture Research Unit (Ccru) developed a series of radical theoretical

All men dream: but not equally. Those who dream by night in the dusty recesses of their minds wake up in the day to find it was vanity, but the dreamers of the day are dangerous men, for they may act their dreams with open eyes, to make it possible.
T.E. Lawrence (1926, *Seven Pillars of Wisdom: A Triumph*)

N. N. Adams, *Terminal Destruction*,
https://doi.org/10.1007/978-3-032-22274-9_7

experiments at Warwick University.[1] Land's philosophical work with Ccru invoked rereadings of Heidegger, Deleuze and Guattari, and Nietzsche, networking theories and perspectives underpinning modern concepts of accelerationism and technocapitalism[2] Theorising also fed into later developments, sometimes grouped retrospectively and somewhat imprecisely, under speculative realism.[3] However, Land's scholarly work with Ccru ended (along with Ccru itself) in the early 2000s.

It is important to state the chronology clearly: Ccru's work precedes the consolidation of speculative realism by more than a decade, and while their materials influenced subsequent philosophical currents, they did not emerge from the same milieu.[4] This chapter centres Ccru's notions of *hyperstition*: theory suggesting fictional narratives comprise positive-feedback circuits that operate as catalysts for reality, conjuring supposed concepts from a fictional plane into the *real*.

Following the i/Acc groundwork of Chapter 6, understanding hyperstition is critical for developing theory as to how the present *decline* of society can be understood through the vector of *immediate modernity* and via the combined lenses of *the beau idéal disconnect*, *immediate modernity's deterritorialised flow paradox*, and Investigatory Accelerationism. Theorising presented in Chapters 2–7 explores the position that capitalist

[1] Periodically the existence of the Ccru collective has been questioned, and at times formally denied by Warwick University. Ccru have acknowledged this by stating: "Ccru is the name on a door in an institution which said of the Ccru that [it] does not, has not, and will never exist" (Ccru, 2017, p. 6).

[2] *Technocapitalism* as used here describes the interconnected rise of technology and capital-linked structuring of society (as discussed in detail within Chapters 2, 3, 5 and 6).

[3] *Speculative realism* describes post-continental philosophy and aims to overcome the limits of correlationism philosophy and human finitude arguments.

[4] Speculative realism coheres as a named movement around the 2007 Goldsmiths conference (Brassier et al., 2007). Ccru's activity (mid-1990s–early 2000s) predates this consolidation; overlaps exist by influence, not contemporaneity. While Ccru's activity throughout the 1990s predates the consolidation of speculative realism as a movement, its influence is unmistakable. Land's early cybernetic and anti-correlationist writings alongside Ccru's experiments in theoryfiction provided conceptual foundations that later philosophers, including Quentin Meillassoux, Ray Brassier, Iain Hamilton Grant, and Graham Harman, would formalise under the speculative realism banner from approximately 2007 onwards. Ccru's work thus belongs not to speculative realism proper, but to its prehistory: a proto-speculative formation that extended Deleuze and Guattari's metaphysical materialism into the domains of technology, language, and occulted capital.

hegemony's control circuits are intrinsically self-replicating. Hyperstition offers the framework to understand how this process is actualised in *immediate modernity*. Interrogating Land's[5] theory of hyperstition (HyS) is the primary focus of this chapter. Concepts such as language, time, and control are reinterpreted through an occult-tinged, techno-cultural lens. First, hyperstition is explored as a concept, providing a clarified definition and deconstructing contemporary scholarly use. The origins of hyperstition are then revisited within the writings of William S. Burroughs. Following this, Ccru's original notions of hyperstition linked to Burroughs's works are reinterpreted, as both examples of hyperstition-in-practice and, in Chapter 8, as an interpretive form of *rationalised psychedelic ego death*. Hyperstition as a clarified concept is revealed to be a salient mechanism for conceptualising *The Decline* within *immediate modernity*.

7.1 Hyperstition: Towards a Clarified Understanding

Hyperstition, in its original Ccru formulation, is not simply an inverse of superstition, nor a matter of 'belief producing reality' in a scripted sense. Hyperstition names the process through which fictions acquire enough cultural, affective, or infrastructural traction to become operative within the real (i.e. the real-life material world). HyS represents a positive-feedback mechanism in which narrative constructs, symbols, or speculative models loop through media systems, technical infrastructures, and collective cognition until they precipitate material effects. Where superstition hinges on avoidance and fear, hyperstition operates by propagation: fictions gain velocity as they circulate, drawing virtually powered potentials into actualisation. This dynamic can be interpretively read through Deleuze's actual/virtual distinction (1994); hyperstition activates the virtual: latent potentials, alternative trajectories, unactualised tendencies, and pulls them towards concrete expression via recursive

[5] While this work is officially attributed to Ccru, as was the Ccru trend for collective attribution, various online sources alternatingly attribute this work to either Ccru or only Land. From hereon I refer to *Lemurian time war* as a Ccru work.

circulation.[6] The virtual does not denote the unreal or imaginary; it is a plane of potentiality, a reservoir of tendencies, affects, and relations that can be actualised through encounter and repetition: through *manifestation*. The actual, by contrast, is *what becomes manifest*: the crystallisation of a potential into perceivable form. Hyperstition functions as the circuit between these two registers. Fictional constructs: narratives, memes, speculative ideas all inhabit the virtual, but through circulation, belief, and repetition, they acquire enough density—enough *velocity*—to crossover into the actual. This process operates as a machinic feedback loop between representation and event: the idea generates behaviour, and behaviour substantiates the idea. The Ccru's phrase "hype actually makes things happen" (Ccru, 1998) captures this ontological relay, with fiction acting as a motor. In *immediate modernity*, this dynamic has become infrastructural, but primarily applied to capital. Networked systems amplify virtual signals: rumours, data, speculation into actual market movements, technological innovation, and social affect. Capital itself represents the largest hyperstitional machine created: a recursive system where projected value precedes and produces material reality. Reframed through Deleuze (1994) then, hyperstition describes a process of *immanent actualisation*: a feedback through which collective imagination *engineers* the real. This makes it central to understanding the logics of *immediate modernity*, where futures are continually invoked, monetised, and made tangible through recursive mediations of hype, belief, and code. So: hyperstition is a fiction that *makes itself real*, a positive-feedback circuit that includes culture as a central component and where the influence of the fictional-real becomes blurred into a singular pulse (Ccru, 2017; Land, 2009).

One of the clearest (and most often cited) demonstrations of hyperstition-in-practice is the rise of *cyberspace*. The author William Gibson coined the term in *Burning Chrome* (1982) and later *Neuromancer* (1984) to name a virtual, networked plane populated by artificial intelligences: a world that, at the time, existed only in fiction. Yet, "cyberspace" escaped its narrative frame, embedding itself in public vocabulary and eventually becoming the default descriptor for early internet life. Here, the fiction arrives first and the infrastructure follows. This is hyperstition at work: a speculative construct gaining enough traction to organise

[6] In Deleuzian terms, the virtual is not unreal but a field of potential—a reservoir, operating in parallel to 'the real' and requiring activation to instigate 'crossover' (Deleuze, 1994).

real behaviours, technical development, and collective imagination. The boundary between the fictional and the real does not dissolve so much as reverberate, merging into a single continuum where ideas migrate, stick, and materialise.

Exploring relevant use of hyperstition in blended fictions and philosophy is important to situate this chapter in context. Reza Negarestani's speculative realism novel *Cyclonopedia: Complicity with Anonymous Materials* (2021) presents a salient example, with Negarestani himself voicing Land's philosophical influence upon his work: "I remember, in 1997, I discovered [Nick] Land" (Negarestani, 2024). *Cyclonopedia* pioneers a modern concept of theoryfiction[7] operating to reshape novelistic literary boundaries by delineating a seemingly stable series of speculative ideas, before presenting opposing concepts and fictions that reconstruct these. At the heart of *Cyclonopedia* lies the motif of oil, framed not simply as a natural resource, but as a living, conspiratorial force: *the blood of the earth*. Negarestani recasts oil as an anchor-point for shaping reality, a near-sentient agent that conjures geotemporal influence over the trajectory of history, past and contemporary geopolitics, and environmental collapse. This reimagining transforms oil into a construct beyond a definable commodity, with *oil* transmuting to represent the protagonist within humanity's unfolding narrative. Alongside notions of power, the setting of *The Middle East* is presented within *Cyclonopedia* as an evolving geopolitical landscape, a literary mirror within which entropy and conflict exist together as historic consequences, but also represent forces that conjure their own agency: sourcing power from the region itself in ways that challenge historical 'knowns'. Such contradictory visions question 'real-world' interpretations of global events, suggesting a deeper, self-perpetuating logic at work underneath the surface of contemporary geopolitics and the documentation of geopolitical histories. This instability is compounded by the narration of the novel by the protagonist: Dr. Hamid Parsani. Parsani's esoteric theories and conspiracies craft another narrative layer within *Cyclonopedia*, intersecting with the power and historical frames presented, leading to a blurring of the boundaries between *what we know* and *what we believe*. As the novel evolves, Parsani becomes part of this hyperstitional mechanism, leading the reader, like a

[7] Theoryfiction operates as a narrative–theoretical method in which speculative form becomes a generative device, enabling concepts to be produced, tested, and reconfigured through fiction rather than confined to conventional analytic exposition.

guide, through a narrative that feels like it may imminently transform to depict a factual reality, representing a real-world explanation for evolving global energy-tensions.

Negarestani's text performs hyperstition rather than simply describing it. *Cyclonopedia* constructs an ontological engine within which oil, capital, and narrative continually fold back upon one another. Oil symbolises more than a metaphor for global power; it functions as a sentient lubricant of history, a living medium through which geopolitical flows are both sustained and destabilised. This reanimation of 'matter as agent' echoes Ccru's claim that matter itself is caught in feedback. The novel's parasitic narrativity: the stories within stories, fragments within reports, all model how fictions circulate and acquire autonomy. *Cyclonopedia* therefore occupies the same operational terrain as Ccru's *Lemurian time war*: both mobilise writing as technics, as a kind of contagion that infects and reorganises real-world perceptions. Negarestani's use of oil as a conspiratorial substance prefigures *actual* transformations in the immediate global energy climate, where energy infrastructures, petrocapitalism, and planetary extraction operate as economic systems but also as speculative frameworks that sustain collective investments: *beliefs* in growth and progress. This recursive structure—fiction feeding into infrastructure—demonstrates hyperstition's performative potency. The novel symbolically *represents* these forces while concurrently *producing them*, rendering geopolitics a feedback system of intersecting myth-matter. By framing oil as a hyperstitional agent, *Cyclonopedia* collapses the boundaries between material and symbolic economies, anticipating the ways in which modern technocapital mobilises hype and speculation to produce real effects. The novel's recursive narrative structure becomes a practical demonstration of hyperstition's power: fiction operating as a system that rewires the real.

In a similar literary vein, Tom McCarthy's novel *Satin Island* (2015) employs hyperstition as a central plot device. *Satin Island* follows 'U', a corporate anthropologist tasked with creating "The Great Report", the "last word" on the human condition that encapsulates the current cultural Zeitgeist as the indomitable spirit of the present modernity (p. 16). This assignment becomes an obsessive quest for U, as he searches, with mounting freneticism, for hidden patterns and connections within social reality.

U's pursuit of 'The Great Report' provides the novel's hyperstitional dynamic: a fiction that acquires enough interpretive and affective density to begin shaping the very reality it seeks to describe. U's fixation on seemingly unconnected events: mysterious deaths, infrastructural failures, the opaque and never-explicated 'Koob-Sassen' project, mirrors the hyperstitional logic found in *Cyclonopedia*: the sense that submerged forces, networks, or entities exert a covert influence on history and material reality. As U increasingly reads the world through this lens, conjecture begins to function as evidence, speculation loops back into perception and the fiction gains traction. This pull is central to hyperstition theory: ideas do not merely *represent* the world but begin to organise it. In *Satin Island* this position is exacerbated by the conditions of a digital-information hegemony; U is saturated by images, datasets, fragments, feeds, all symbolic debris that blur the line between documentation and simulation. Reality becomes experienced at a remove, as if mediated through a permanent filter of algorithmic noise. What emerges is a world that feels hyperconstructed: not intrinsically false, but engineered via circulating narratives, models, and conjectures that take on the coherence of truth through repetition and scale. The novel parallels *Cyclonopedia* not only in mood but in mechanism. Where Negarestani uses oil as the occult engine driving geopolitical and ontological instability, *Satin Island* installs 'The Report' as its organising myth, the empty centre around which U's reality begins to distort. As Grewe-Volpp (2019) notes, the recurring motif of 'an oil spill' renders *Satin Island* a petrofiction, with U "search[ing] for the meaning of oil in a thoroughly digitised and mediated world, in which his grasp of the world depends on pixelated images" (p. 1). This parallel reinforces the novel's core tension: U's world appears somehow 'less real', thinned-out and over-mediated, yet increasingly catalogued by the very fictions he and others circulate. *Satin Island* stages hyperstition as a lived condition of *immediate modernity*, one in which the distinction between narrative and world collapses into a recursive system of belief, circulation, and affective digital capture.

A related, tangible, and real-world contemporary illustration of hyperstition can be found in the recent history of Aberdeen's North Sea oil economy. During the post-2014 downturn, when falling Brent crude prices destabilised the city's long-standing industrial identity, waves of speculative optimism periodically circulated; rumours of an imminent 'upturn' promised rebounds in exploration, or impending investment cycles. These claims were rarely grounded in material indicators, yet their circulation alone generated temporary behavioural shifts: contractors hired in anticipation, training programmes reopened, recruitment pipelines flickered back to life. The belief preceded the conditions it imagined. For a brief period, the narrative of resurgence acted as if it were already true, animating organisational decisions, labour movements, and market behaviour despite the absence of structural recovery. When the promised upturn failed to materialise, the hyperstitional arc collapsed, revealing how the city had been collectively moved by a fiction that produced tangible effects before dissolving. In this sense, Aberdeen's petrofiction is emblematic of hyperstition's wider logic in *immediate modernity*: stories of the future do not merely describe possible worlds; they actively shape present conduct, structuring hope, labour, and investment in ways that materialise the very conditions they anticipate, even when those conditions ultimately vanish.

A further example of hyperstition appears in the emergence of Bitcoin. Before Bitcoin was a functioning technical infrastructure, 'Bitcoin' existed primarily as a white paper, a speculative vision authored under a pseudonym, and an online community's projected belief in a novel monetary paradigm. The fiction: an autonomous, trustless, non-state currency, gathered momentum through circulation: forums, mailing lists, early adopters, and speculative narratives about decentralised finance. This narrative feedback loop preceded its material stability; so, belief had to accrete before the system could scale. Once the fiction reached critical mass, it 'bootstrapped[8]' itself into the real as an economic and geopolitical force, shaping policy, markets, and technological development. This is hyperstition in Ccru's strict sense: a recursive fiction that, through hype, technical uptake, and social contagion, engineers the conditions of its own actualisation.

Drawing on the above examples from 'fictions' and 'reality', Fig. 7.1 presents a clarified framework detailing hyperstition-in-practice.

[8] I employ this terminology as a nod to Ccru's use of the term. Bootstrapping, in the Ccru sense, is the process by which a system or entity brings itself into being through its own operations, generating the conditions of its own existence in a self-propelling, self-intensifying loop (Ccru, 2017).

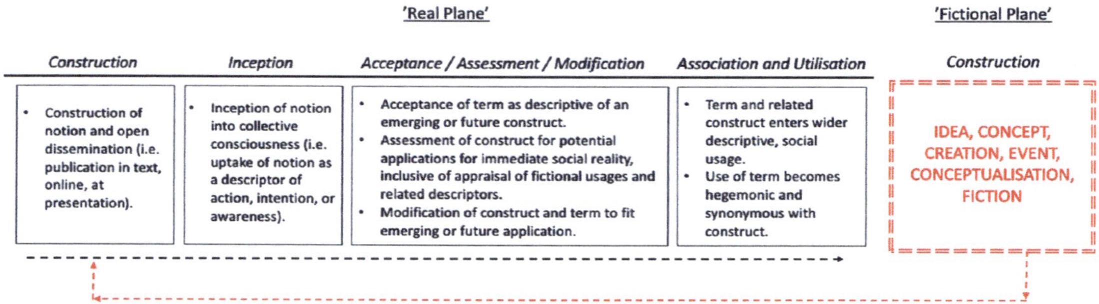

Fig. 7.1 Framework for conceptualising hyperstitional influence factoring Land's 'positive-feedback loop' (Land, 2009). *Explanatory note* Feedback circuits are shown in red. Fictions are shaped by reality and realities are shaped by fictions: the first four boxes represent societal processes within the 'real'—the development of new concepts and ideas and their social uptake. Box five represents the fictional plane, occurring both before and after the development of social processes, yet constructing direct or retrospective influence that shapes social processes. Thus, the feedback circuit could be considered 'positive'. All five components of the circuit are 'live', each influencing the other with the direction of influence always moving both ways in a mutual framework of support (dual *feedforward* and *feedback* mechanisms)

7.2 Existing Hyperstition Research

Some scholars analyse hyperstition. Srnicek and Williams (2017) frame HyS as a driver of accelerationist change, where speculative ideas become tangible through collective belief and action, via conceptual innovation, interface design, adaptive action, and visionary narratives. Parisi (2017) extends this by emphasising gender and alienation, illustrating using Xenofeminism how hyperstitional narratives disrupt conventional notions of identity and existence, enabling radical reinterpretations of self and others. Across both perspectives, HyS functions as a cultural and conceptual tool, melding fiction with reality to challenge established frameworks and generate new socio-political and personal possibilities. Other research frames hyperstition as an interpretative, theoretical platform for examining social phenomena. Mohammed (2024) situates HyS within the Anthropocene, employing HyS as a 'storytelling against hope' framework to shape ecological consciousness. Drawing on melancholy motifs, Mohammed argues HyS can construct sustainability narratives that encourage societies to consider long-term environmental impacts, echoing Burroughs' use of HyS in *The Ghost Lemurs of Madagascar*, where fiction directly engages with real-world ecological concerns. Similarly, Mellamphy (2015) positions humans as vessels for hyperstitional enactment, drawing on Kodwo Eshun's theoretical work[9] to show how speculative futures can be integrated into the present. Mellamphy's later work, extended through notions of Hyperstitching (Mellamphy & Mellamphy, 2020), emphasises how HyS 'stitches together' normally disconnected concepts via fictional narrative, disrupting entrenched hegemonies and enabling alternative modes of social and ecological engagement:

> Hyperstitions […] are sorcerous operations that involve the rapprochement of elements that do not normally go or have not normally belonged together but which have the effects of transmuting perceived reality and norms of culture. (p. 6)

[9] Eshun has also been associated with Ccru.

Zeeuw and Gekker (2023) explore HyS via the phenomenon of conspiracy fictioning in the context of QAnon.[10] They argue QAnon operates as a form of live-action role-playing (LARP). Within QAnon online spaces, fictional narratives are performed alongside established facets of reality, smoothing out boundaries between reality and fiction, as online 'actors' engage in a structure of mutual belief-supports. Hybridised performances allow facets of fiction to be amalgamated into reality via their attachment to established norms, thus increasing their 'believability'.

Finally, *Ludic Dreaming: How to Listen Away from Contemporary Technoculture* (Cecchetto et al., 2017) presents hyperstition as an experiential practice rather than a purely theoretical or investigative concept. The authors describe how participants are invited to 'listen away' from conventional cultural and identity frameworks, using lucid dreaming to engage with fictional narratives and reframe dreams as data. This approach encourages the exploration of alternative modes of existence, emphasising the ritualistic and transformative potential of HyS, and resonates with the psychedelic and performative dimensions highlighted by Ccru, while connecting conceptually with the ecological, speculative, and identity-focused work of Zeeuw and Gekker, Mellamphy, Parisi, and Mohammed.

7.3 William S. Burroughs: The Ghost Lemurs of Madagascar

Hyperstition was most formalised by Ccru in their work *Lemurian time war* (Ccru, 2017). The report discusses a novella by William S. Burroughs: *The Ghost Lemurs of Madagascar* (abbreviated hereafter as GLOM) as the archetypal example of hyperstition-in-practice. The following section first outlines and deconstructs Burroughs' original novella. Then follows a comparison of this against a radical interpretation of the GLOM's narrative by Ccru, which argues for GLOM as an invocation of hyperstition.

Burroughs' *The Ghost Lemurs of Madagascar* offers a detailed exploration of history, speculative fiction, and ecological allegory, interwoven with parallel symbolic critiques of human exploitation, colonialism, and

[10] A far-right political and conspiracy movement operating mostly online. For an overview see Garry et al. (2021).

environmental degradation. First published in *Omni* magazine in 1987, the narrative reflects Burroughs' unique experimental style and engagements with themes of non-linear temporalities, identity, and human-nature relationships. GLOM, like much of Burroughs' later works, is infused with the surrealist and psychedelic undertones of Burroughs' literary voice, reflecting Burroughs' fascination with altered states of consciousness as a vehicle for interrogating both *the self* and the position of *the human* within the natural world (Burroughs, 1987). GLOM also represents a theoryfiction; components of the story have elements rooted in real-world occurrences and histories, but these are blended with fictions to create a confusing, blurred depiction of peoples, places, and events.

At the centre of GLOM is the character of Captain Mission, a (supposed-fictional) late-seventeenth century seafarer, positioned as founder of the libertarian pirate colony of *Libertaria* in Madagascar. Burroughs outlines Mission's story via a fantastical lens, fusing partial historical facts with Burroughs' own countercultural ethos: colliding ideals of equality, freedom, and anti-violence against encroachments of human greed and exploitation. Mission's engagement with Madagascar's natural environment, particularly the lemurs, becomes emblematic of the fragile balance between humanity and nature, one that Burroughs, drawing on his broader ecological concerns, positions as increasingly endangered by linked colonial and capitalist forces.

Mission originates from a wealthy background and is said to have excelled academically, enrolling in the University of Angers in the late-1700s, studying logic, mathematics, and humanities. After graduating, Mission takes up a commission aboard the war vessel *Victoire*, rumoured to have been commanded by his distant cousin and furnished with an extensive armoury of thirty cannons. The ship is positioned as a formidable combat vessel. Mission sails with *Victoire* first to Naples, and then on to Rome, where *Victoire* engages and defeats two vessels before crossing the Atlantic, before being engaged in the Caribbean by the vessel *Winchelsea*, commanded by one Captain Opium Jones. After a prolonged skirmish, which leads to the death of Captain Jones of the *Victoire*, the second captain and three lieutenants, Mission takes command of the remaining men to stage a victory and capture the *Winchelsea*. The fate of Captain Opium Jones is unclear, but with the captured English vessel and crew in tow, Mission guides both the *Victoire* and *Winchelsea*, through the Guinea coast and West Africa, stopping to lend firepower support to the Queen of Johanna[11]'s efforts to capture the island of Mohéli (Mwali[12]). They then traverse the Mozambique coast and anchor, settling permanently on the Western Madagascan coast where Mission founds the libertarian colony *Libertaria*.

The utopian colony *Libertaria* is ruled by Mission via a set of articles akin to "the French and American revolutionaries of the late eighteenth century [but preceding these] by more than sixty years" (Burroughs, 1987, p. 3). Mission's laws reject capital punishment, slavery and imprisonment and adopt laissez-faire, pro-individualist attitudes to religion and sexuality.

After an unknown passage of time on *Libertaria*, and following an expedition led by Mission to explore a neighbouring island, several sailors drink rum punch upon the shores. Mission and his men are marooned when changeable seas drift the *Victoire* beyond rescuable distance: the ship grounding upon coastal rocks. Mission and his expedition are now trapped on this new island, which they name *Lemuria*.

Lemuria is a legendary locale: a mythical island inhabited by numerous large, unusual, and alluring lemurs, descriptions of which dominate GLOM. The concept of *Lemuria* has been central to various real-world mythologies and 'theories of lost geographies' throughout history, associated with past civilisations and ancient mysteries (Ramaswamy, 2004). In Burroughs's GLOM, *Lemuria* is portrayed as a remote, enigmatic island upon which strange and unexplainable events unfold. Within these 'stories-within-stories' the motif of the lemur is ever-present, with lemurs seemingly guarding over the island, communicating via symbolism and ritual with Mission's crew, and influencing the passage of time upon *Lemuria*. Such occurrences present the lemurs as phantom-like creatures; as Burroughs points out: "The word *lemur* means *ghost* in the native language"[13] (1987, p. 24). Upon *Lemuria*, Mission's articles of

[11] This reference is a temporal curiosity of Burroughs' work. The Queen of Joanna, the nominal queen of Castile, was, in reality, born in 1479, reigning from 1504 (Castile) until her death in 1555. This is at least two centuries prior to the events depicted in Burroughs' work and examined in the Ccru report. It is possible Burroughs is referring to a different Queen of Joanna, and indeed the spelling differs: Johanna (Burroughs, 1987, p. 24) vs. the 'Joanna' of historical record.

[12] An island situated at the Northern mouth of the Mozambique Channel, located between the islands of Comoros (North) and Mayotte (South).

[13] In GLOM, it is unclear what the local or indigenous language of *Lemuria* is.

law prohibit the killing of 'ghosts' (aka lemurs) with Mission depicted as possessing a great love for and affinity with the lemurs inhabiting the island and a desire to protect their existence at all costs.

The lemurs are pivotal to the GLOM. They operate not simply as symbols of Madagascar's biodiversity but as *ghostly entities* networked to deeper, psychedelic realities. Lemurs represent liminal beings, straddling boundaries between visibility and invisibility, life and death, the physical and the metaphysical. The lemurs' ability to transition between states of existence echoes Burroughs' long-standing fascination with the mind's capacity to transcend material reality through altered states, often induced via psychedelics. Burroughs' engagement with psychoactive substances like yagé and opium, which he wrote about extensively, particularly in *The Yage Letters* (1963, see Burroughs & Ginsberg, 2008), is subtly echoed in GLOM's hallucinatory tone and literary depictions of nature as something concurrently tangible and spectral: a world on the fringes of known reality, but also a gateway into an unexplored and uncharted world. However, it is implied one must have the right guide to traverse this unknown path.

Through these frames, Captain Mission's relationship with the enigmatic lemurs is portrayed as one of reverence, but also of psycho-spiritual fascination. In contrast to the conventionally human characters of GLOM, all bound by the rules of time, mortality, and material concerns, *Lemuria*'s lemurs embody a reality adrift from capital and *desire*-led structures. They share a form of collective consciousness that Burroughs associated with psychedelic experiences—a state where time is no longer linear, and where the boundaries of self and environment converge. This reality-divergent perception speaks to Burroughs' writings on psychedelics, through which he sought to define what he terms a higher, more authentic reality, absent from the distortions imposed by societal hegemonies (Lees, 2017). Burroughs infuses this idyllic-psychedelic sensibility throughout the GLOM narrative, spotlighting disjunctions between the timeless and tranquil existence of the lemurs and the destructive culture imposed by humans from the point they arrive on *Lemuria*, disrupting and fracturing the lemurs' perfect equilibrium. Mission's utopian project initially seeks to align itself with nature, and Mission's enforcement of definitive laws against killing lemurs symbolises an attempt to protect an unspoilt, quasi-spiritual natural order. Further, it is implied that Mission's study of the lemurs is to learn from their way of life—the lemurs operating as metaphysical guides that can define new perceptions of reality, and indeed reveal new ways of *being* to Mission and his men. However, as the narrative progresses, it becomes clear that human nature, and by connection, human time, cannot be extricated from mortal cycles of greed, violence, and exploitation. Mission's utopian visions of *Libertaria/Lemuria* implode as the human characters revert to selfishness and disregard for the natural world, eventually spiralling to circumvent the sacred protections of the lemurs that Mission upheld as edict.

The pivotal moment in GLOM occurs when one of Mission's settlers kills a lemur (on *Lemuria*) for stealing a mango. This violent act, which is devoid of regret, marks the point at which Mission's utopian ideal achieves total collapse, exposing the inherent contradiction between the human aspiration for true freedom and the intrinsic destructive impulses that accompany this drive. Here, Burroughs' critique of the human condition emerges, as the colonial project that sought to impose order and progress is shown to be fundamentally incapable of escaping the very forces of domination and exploitation it has ostensibly been constructed to resist and interrupt. As opposed to realising a divorce from human impulses of destruction, Mission and his men have simply transferred these impulses to a previously unspoiled locale. In GLOM, lemurs are not simply endangered species requiring conservation; rather, they symbolise an ancient, uncolonised format of existence that resists the human compulsion to dominate and exploit. This psychedelic, utopian vision is presented as an alternative to the destructive *drives*[14] of human history: a glimpse of a world that operates via different rules, different *desires*, and one within which the lemurs are attuned to a worldly rhythm far removed from the capital-led pursuits and interlinked corruption and violence that structure human time. Madagascar, with its isolated evolutionary history, becomes a microcosm for the fragility of social ecosystems under human pressure. The lemurs' existence, spanning sixty million years, is juxtaposed against the relatively brief period of human habitation, during which time nearly half of Madagascar's lemur species have been driven to extinction. This destruction, Burroughs suggests, is not only resultant of human greed or short-sightedness, but confirms a deeper, more fundamental social failing: humanity's inability to transcend its temporal and material limitations, even via supposed resistance through attempted utopian pursuits.

[14] I discuss in Chapter 5 the use of *Drives* against the concept of Trieb.

Mission's own failure, both as a leader and as a human being, underscores this point. Mission's vision of an egalitarian society, free from the corrupting influences of the outside world, collapses because it is built on the same hegemonic temporal and material structuring foundations that underpin all human societies: the pursuit of competitive capital. Thus, the core metaphor of Burroughs' GLOM is that human society, while structured per established capital hegemony, is forever doomed to eventually fail, as the self-replicating DNA of the modern human condition is bound to self-destruction.

Burroughs challenges the reader with the existential consequences of this failure. The extinction of the lemurs symbolises not only the loss of a unique species but the delegitimisation of alternative ways of being in the world, ways that Burroughs came to understand as vital to the survival of both humanity and the planet. Burroughs' invocation of the lemurs as psychic entities, able to shift between metaphorical visible and invisible states, exists as a metaphor beyond a fantastical element of GLOM; it is a commentary on the potential for different forms of consciousness, untethered from the destructive forces of human time and history, to offer a glimpse of a more harmonious and fulfilling worldly existence.

Despite the mystical and psychedelic undertones of the GLOM narrative, Burroughs does not present an easy resolution. The ghost lemurs, much like the psychedelic insights that Burroughs often describes as fleeting and difficult to grasp, remain elusive. They offer a vision of what could have been: an existence unburdened by the demands of material survival and exploitation, but one that is ultimately lost to the inescapable human condition. Burroughs' closing plea in GLOM for the conservation of Madagascar's lemurs foregrounds real-world ecological urgency, yet carries the narrative's characteristic sense of inevitable failure. For Burroughs, the lemurs' extinction signals a broader existential crisis, reflecting humanity's inability to overcome the pro-capital forces that ensure the collapse of counter-hegemonic utopian visions.

7.4 Ccru: Lemurian Time War Report

Ccru's *Lemurian time war* (Ccru, 2017) offers a unique interpretation of Burroughs' GLOM, situating the story within the labyrinthine framework of hyperstition theory and masterfully networking together elements of theoryfiction. GLOM is viewed as both a catalyst and a record of metaphysical and temporal conflict; Ccru's report locates Burroughs as a key figure in an occult time war, where Burroughs' writings interact with temporal anomalies and control systems.

Ccru's account begins by introducing William Kaye as 'an insider' who provided sensitive information about an organisation called The Board to Ccru. According to Kaye (as told by Ccru), Burroughs' *The Ghost Lemurs of Madagascar* is far from being a conventional work of fiction. Instead, the novella is claimed to represent an exact and decisive influence upon a real-life Captain Mission, the same eighteenth century pirate who founded the utopian colony *Libertaria* on Madagascar, and is presented as a semi-fictional character by Burroughs. Ccru detail that Kaye claimed he had discovered an ancient illustrated transcript of Burroughs' text, meticulously inscribed by Mission himself, thereby demonstrating a rift in time that directly links the two figures across temporalities, and indeed across factual and fictitious existences. This time anomaly, or *spiral templex*, was identified by The Board as a matter of grave concern, as spirals are destabilising forces that disrupt the predictable, controlled flow of time. Ccru connect this time rift with their broader notion of hyperstition, where Burroughs' fictional writing becomes an inciting agent for reality. The report delves into Burroughs' fixations with occult and esoteric practices and fascinations with sorcery, dreams, and fiction. Ccru draw parallels between Burroughs' GLOM and the concept of viruses in another of Burroughs' works: *Ah Pook is Here*, where Burroughs' writing represents a form of viral contamination that spreads and alters reality itself (Burroughs, 1982). GLOM is suggested to be more than a fictional story, representing a hyperstitional artefact that both documents and instigates real-world temporal disturbances: a *hyperstitional object*.[15]

In a parallel to Kaye's alleged discovery of an original GLOM manuscript, *Lemurian time war* describes Kaye's recounting of Burroughs' own discovery of an old picture book in the New York Vysparov private library in 1958, said to be owned by one ex-military captain Peter Vysparov, founder of The Vysparov Collection.[16] This book would later become *The Ghost Lemurs of Madagascar*, a text that Burroughs was yet to write but that Mission had already authored

[15] A hyperstitional object is a fiction that becomes real by shaping the conditions of its own emergence, a text or artefact whose circulation alters behaviour, belief, and infrastructure such that the world retroactively reorganises itself to make the object *true*.

[16] This author was unable to verify the authenticity, nor existence of this archive, although several online-based mentions and discussions of this were located.

centuries earlier. The suggestion here is either that Mission penned the original text, somehow manipulating Burroughs' later 1980s authorship, or that Burroughs penned the original text, and that this generated retroactive temporal influence over the actions of Mission, with Mission then penning a version of GLOM in his own temporality of the 1700s. Kaye goes on to cite his knowledge of a board, perhaps the same board that Burroughs' GLOM story alludes to having watched over Mission during his escape to solitude within the jungle and his engagements with psychedelics on *Lemuria*. The Board considers the existence of this parallel copy of Burroughs' work a matter of the gravest concern, and evidence of a *demonstrable time rift*. This fragmenting of timeline(s) is referred to as a time-spiral: spirals always having loose ends compared with the 'closed' structure of time-loops.

Immediately following this alleged discovery, Ccru argue Burroughs experienced a profound *time-trauma*, entering a trance state where he was transported forward into his own future, while simultaneously recalling his life as Captain Mission. This 'temporal rupture' enduringly affected Burroughs, driving him to develop the 'cut-up' and 'fold-in' writing techniques that would later become central to his authorship. These techniques, per Kaye, were designed to disrupt the *pre-recorded universe* and to subvert the linearity of time, encouraging a 'breaking free' from the control of the One God Universe (OGU)—a monolithic reality structure that Burroughs actively sought to escape through his writings. Ccru articulate Burroughs' role in a larger *magical war* against the OGU: a system that imposes a singular, pre-recorded reality. The OGU is depicted as a control programme that governs reality through the manipulation of time and language. Thus, Burroughs' writing—per Ccru—represents a wilful act of resistance against this hegemony. By employing cut-up and experimental writing procedures, Burroughs aimed to fracture the closed loops of time by resisting predictability, striving to generate new *spiral* realities beyond the looping controls of the OGU.

Importantly, Ccru argue the figure of the lemur is central to understanding the OGU temporal conflict. Within GLOM, lemurs exist outside of linear time and operate as symbols of resistance against temporal control. Burroughs portrays lemurs as *psychic amphibians* capable of slipping in and out of visibility, embodying alternative modes of existence that challenge the OGU's authority over reality. Ccru spotlight Burroughs' relationship with cats and lemurs, linking his growing obsession with these animals in the 1980s to his deeper disillusionment with human sexuality and *The Venusian Conspiracy*: a theme present in much of his later work. *The Venusian Conspiracy* reflects Burroughs' recurring exploration of control systems, power structures, and resistance to oppression, with Burroughs often drawing on science fiction imagery, like alien conspiracies or interstellar forces, to locate the real pervasive and insidious mechanisms of capitalist controls embedded in society through the vehicle of fiction, facilitating deeper metaphorical explorations. *The Venusian Conspiracy* operates as an overarching metaphor for hierarchical societal systems, whether political, class-oriented, cultural, or technological, that serve to dominate and control humanity (Burroughs, 1983). This aligns with Burroughs' deep-rooted distrust of centralised authority and his focus on personal and collective liberation. Ccru position Captain Mission and Burroughs as *anachronistic contemporaries*, bound together by the temporal distortions caused by the lemurs and their connection to the lost Lemurian time. This entanglement between Burroughs and Mission represents a deeper hyperstitional process where the boundaries between author and character, past and future, reality and fiction, dissolve. The lemurs, as creatures who predate humanity by millions of years, serve as a conduit for this temporal slippage, linking Burroughs and Mission in a shared struggle against the OGU's control over time and representing—in GLOM—symbols of freedom from motifs of *The Venusian Conspiracy*. Yet, ultimately this freedom fails to be realised, with Mission's men returning to established, programmed processes of hegemony by destroying the freedom-potentials of the lemurs through attempting to dominate *Lemuria*'s idyllic reality and the lemurs themselves. Thus—for Ccru—it is equally humanity's destruction impulse that is hyperstitional, alongside Burroughs' efforts to escape scripted reality.

Ccru ultimately position *The Ghost Lemurs of Madagascar* as a hyperstitional intervention in an ongoing temporal war. Burroughs' writing becomes a weapon against the OGU's reality programme, with each textual act operating as a sorcerous disruption of imposed temporal order. The Board's efforts to seal the rift opened by Burroughs/Captain Mission are framed as failures, as Burroughs' work continues to leak into reality, unsettling linear time and generating new spaces of resistance. The lemurs—literal, symbolic, and metaphysical—form the core of this resistance. Their capacity to exist outside time and move between visibility and invisibility aligns them with Burroughs' wider project of escaping linear temporality and its attendant control structures. For Ccru, the lemurs are not simply endangered creatures but agents of metaphysical and metaphorical disturbance, posing an existential threat to the OGU's programme and the broader architectures of social control.

7.5 Reinterpreting Burroughs and the Ccru Report

Hyperstition, as it circulates through Burroughs' GLOM and Ccru's *Lemurian time war* report, unsettles any clean separation between fiction and reality. Instead, HyS frames fiction-reality as co-produced within a continuous semiotic circuit: a positive-feedback pulse from which narratives do not simply reflect the world but actively instigate its construction. In *The Ghost Lemurs of Madagascar*, Burroughs mobilises esoteric motifs and metaphorical intensities to collapse the boundary between speculative narrative and ecological crisis. The text works hyperstitionally: it provokes the reader to confront the material precarity of Madagascar's lemurs alongside the wider vulnerabilities structuring the human condition. Ccru extend this logic by accentuating hyperstition's temporal implications, particularly its retrocausal tendency—effects looping back to generate their own origins. Their insertion of a supposed 1958 encounter involving Burroughs, Peter Vysparov, and an earlier iteration of GLOM operates as a deliberate hyperstitional mechanism. It dramatises the altered states, temporal glitches, and near-hallucinatory fractures that emerge when narrative and time begin to fold—to *pulse*—into one another. This scene makes explicit hyperstition's capacity to destabilise linear temporality and the fixed, coherent subject that relies upon it. While hyperstition is demonstrably real, both as a theoretical device and as a practical, operational force, Ccru's suggestion that Burroughs literally encountered his future text in the Vysparov archive represents a pointedly excessive version of the theoretical loop Ccru are mapping. The comparison to Gibson's pre-realisation of *cyberspace* is apt, showing how speculative fictions can prefigure (and sometimes accelerate) technological emergence. Yet, even with the coherence of Ccru's construction and the seductive strangeness of their GLOM interpretation, there remains a risk: framing hyperstition primarily as a quasi-occult temporal rupture may constrain its broader value as a critical lens for understanding how narratives produce, shape, and disturb the social world.

7.6 Functional Efforts to Invoke Hyperstition

A useful alternative way to read Ccru's hyperstition is to recognise that their report, much like Burroughs' GLOM, functions as a temporal experiment designed to test whether a fiction can make itself real. The text is populated with unverifiable, and likely fictional, elements: possibly invented scholars such as Dr Echidna Stillwell[17] and her supposed ethnographies; Peter Vysparov and his New York rare literature archive; and the (semi-fabricated?) exploits of Captain Mission and Captain Opium Jones (Ccru, 2017). If a researcher were to take these claims at face value, citing them as factual without sufficient scrutiny or verification, then these fictions would, in effect, be conjured into existence. They would cross from the imaginary into the accepted record. In doing so, they would enact hyperstition's retrocausal logic: the report's fabricated past begins to shape the future, and the future uptake of these details loops back to validate their supposed historical presence. Within a linear frame, a later event retroactively reorganises an earlier one, demonstrating hyperstition's functional capacity to make fictions real. Ccru appear at times to explicitly recognise and reference this position:

> According to the tenets of Hyperstition, there is no difference in principle between a universe, a religion, and a hoax. All involve an engineering of manifestation, or practical fiction, that is ultimately unworthy of belief. Nothing is true, because everything is under production. **Because the future is a fiction, it has a more intense reality than either the present or the past** (Ccru, 2017, p. 9). [Bolding added]

There is, in fact, some tangible evidence for reading Ccru's report as an experimental paradigm: a deliberate attempt to *invoke* hyperstition rather than simply *theorise* it. Some online sources now cite figures such as Peter Vysparov and Dr. Echidna Stillwell as if they were historically real, despite there being no verifiable records of their existence outside Ccru's own materials. This uncritical repetition effectively retrocausalises the fiction: present-day references grant legitimacy to characters who only 'exist'

[17] Much online discourse, communiques, and materials are available linking to Dr Stillwell and her alleged ethnographic studies. However, none of these are verifiable, and exist in a quasi-reality within digital spaces: sometimes being referred to as fact, at other times fiction, at other times in combinations of both. Thus, these are hyperstitional constructs in themselves.

within Ccru/Burroughs narratives, thereby manufacturing a lineage of influence that appears to flow backwards into the report's purported historical frame. In doing so, these later citations transform Ccru's inventions into quasi-factual entities: an enactment of hyperstition in practice. The report does not merely describe how hyperstition works; it performs it, operating as a proof-of-concept that tests the theory's limits by seeding fictions that subsequently acquire external affirmation. I contend this was likely the underlying intention behind *Lemurian time war*, yet this hyperstitional function remains largely unacknowledged within existing scholarship on esotericism, Ccru's history, and theoretical treatments of hyperstition.

References

Brassier, R., Grant, I. H., Harman, G., & Meillassoux, Q. (2007). Speculative realism. In R. Mackay (Ed.), *Collapse: Philosophical research and development* (Vol. III, pp. 307–450). Urbanomic.

Burroughs, W. S. (1982) *Ah Pook is here and other texts*. Riverrun Press.

Burroughs, W. S. (1983). *The place of dead roads*. Penguin.

Burroughs, W. S. (1987). The Ghost Lemurs of Madagascar. *Omni Science Fiction, 103*, 48–54.

Burroughs, W. S., & Ginsberg, A. (2008). *The yage letters redux*. Penguin.

Ccru [De Rosario, M]. (1998). *Apocalypse—Been in effect?* Cybernetic Culture Research Unit. http://www.ccru.net/syzygy/apoc.htm

Ccru. (2017). *Writings 1997–2003*. Urbanomic.

Cecchetto, D., Couroux, M., Hiebert, T., & Priest, E. (2017). *Ludic dreaming: How to listen away from contemporary technoculture*. Bloomsbury Publishing.

Deleuze, G. (1994). *Difference and repetition*. Columbia University Press.

Garry, A., Walther, S., Rukaya, R., & Mohammed, A. (2021). QAnon conspiracy theory: Examining its evolution and mechanisms of radicalization. *Journal for Deradicalization, 26*, 152–216.

Gibson, W. (1982). *Burning Chrome. Omni*. [Online Archive].

Gibson, W. (1984). *Neuromancer*. Harper Voyager.

Grewe-Volpp, C. (2019). Oil as matter, oil as discourse: Tom McCarthy's Satin Island. *Green Letters, 23*(2), 141–151.

Land, N. (2009). *'Hyperstition': An introduction*. Delphi Carstens Interviews Nick Land. https://www.orphandriftarchive.com/articles/hyperstition-an-introduction/

Lees, A. J. (2017). William Burroughs: Sailor of the soul. *Journal of Psychoactive Drugs, 49*(5), 385–392.

McCarthy, T. (2015). *Satin Island*. Jonathan Cape.

Mellamphy, D., & Mellamphy, N. B. (2020). Mort à discredit: Otium, Negotium, and the critique of transcendental miserabilism: Bernard Stiegler, disbelief and discredit, volumes I–III. *Parrhesia: A Journal of Critical Philosophy, 34.*

Mellamphy, N. B. (2015). *The three stigmata of Kodwo Eshun: On the human as hyperstition.* Prepared for the new centre course on hyperstition, Fictional Worlds & Possible Futures.

Mohammed, S. (2024). Storying against hope in the anthropocene: On the mechanology of hyperstitions. In A *World Scientific Encyclopedia of Business Storytelling Set 2: Methodologies and Big Data Analysis of Business Storytelling Volume 2: Business Storytelling and Sustainability* (pp. 15–33).

Negarestani, R. (2021). *Cyclonopedia.* LUISS University Press.

Negarestani, R. (2024). *Reza Negarestani discovers the deep object that is Nick Land.* YouTube. https://www.youtube.com/watch?v=CQCqVACdDe4 [Original recording from The New Centre, Seminar Series, Sessions 7 and 8. 2017: *The Draw of the Desert*].

Parisi, L. (2017). Automate sex: Xenofeminism, hyperstition, and alienation. *Futures and Fictions*, 213–248.

Ramaswamy, S. (2004). *The lost land of Lemuria: Fabulous geographies, catastrophic histories.* University of California Press.

Srnicek, N., & Williams, A. (2017). 1. Accelerationism and hyperstition. *Cyclops Journal.*

Zeeuw, D. D., & Gekker, A. (2023). A god-tier LARP? QAnon as conspiracy fictioning. *Social Media+ Society, 9*(1), 20563051231157300. https://doi.org/10.1177/20563051231157300

CHAPTER 8

Hyperstition as Rational Ego Death

All that remains is despair and a future of meaningless tomorrows. But I will never give up.
Wording seen upon a digital artefact within Silent Hill 2 (2001, PlayStation 2 game, directed and developed by Team Silent for Konami Computer Entertainment Tokyo)

Abstract Extending from Chapter 7, and this chapter now locates hyperstition into the psychological register. It asks what it means to maintain a coherent self within recursive symbolic systems. Drawing on psychodynamic perspectives, it proposes *rational ego death*: a cognitive and emotional dissolution produced by uncertain saturation. Subjectivity is no longer narrative but feedback-based, continually reconstructed through loops of signal and affect. Under *immediate modernity*, the self doesn't collapse: it is dispersed.

Keywords Subjectivity · Rational ego death · Feedback · Psychological modernity · William S. Burroughs

Reframing hyperstition in a different context to the theorising in Chapter 7, this time through a psychological lens of sensemaking, is useful, particularly when considering hyperstition as the primary construct from which capitalistic hegemony is perpetrated as forward momentum

N. N. Adams, *Terminal Destruction*,
https://doi.org/10.1007/978-3-032-22274-9_8

within *immediate modernity*. This second, radically different, interpretation of the Ccru report operates at a *psychotheoretical* conceptual level.

The Ccru report contains numerous motifs of structural escapism, linking predominantly to factors that define accepted parameters of reality, which are commonly recognised as unalterable, for example: time and temporality, embodied identity, and foundational sense of self. It is curious that Burroughs' commentary in GLOM discusses an OGU control hegemony, which is primarily centred upon a shadowy board maintaining complete worldly control through their manipulation of time. Time represents one of the elemental principles of society for which human actors have no control over its manipulation, but have total control over how they spend their time and interpretatively construct meaning from this. Equally notable are Burroughs' reflections on time-disruptions within GLOM as a focal plot point, and his placing of emphasis on Captain Mission's experiential perspectives on time-dilation, utilising the literary device of psychedelic substances—Mission's frequent ingestion of "indris crystals"[1] (Burroughs, 1987, p. 30)—to account for Mission dropping in-and-out of different temporalities. Burroughs' references to psychedelics are important: psychedelic substances offer one of the only structural devices by which humans can tangibly manipulate their perceptions of time (Abdelshafy, 2016; Hashkes et al., 2017; Taylor, 2021).

Burroughs himself is well documented to have experimented with various psychedelics, including peyote and ayahuasca (also known as yagé). Ayahuasca particularly intrigued Burroughs (Ruffell et al., 2023; St John, 2016), not only for its mind-altering effects but also for its deep roots in traditional, indigenous shamanic traditions, some of which have been linked to alternative perceptions of time (Bonta, 2018). These themes intersect with readings developed by Fisher, particularly in his *K-Punk* essays (2018) and the unfinished *Acid Communism* manuscript (Fisher & Colquhoun, 2020) where Fisher re-examines Burroughs' fascination with psychedelia as part of a broader cultural struggle between control and liberation. Fisher situates Burroughs within an anti-romantic critique of psychedelic culture: less as a prophet of transcendence than as a diagnostician of culture's susceptibility to capture by capital and

[1] The particulars and origins of these crystals are never fully explained by Burroughs, but they are alluded to as having psychedelic properties.

control systems. On this point, Burroughs' letters to Ginsberg during the early 1960s—later published as *The Yage Letters* (TYL)—document Burroughs' journey through the Amazon in search of the elusive yagé plant. Within TYL, descriptions of ayahuasca are vivid, reflecting both Burroughs' fascination with its capacity to expand consciousness and his awareness of the physical and psychological contradictions altered perceptions can pose. TYL positions Burroughs as perceiving the drug not as a shortcut to enlightenment but as a tool that might offer new insights into human perception, the functions of the human mind, and indeed 'hidden' structures of reality and structural order (Burroughs & Ginsberg, 2008).

Burroughs' juxtaposed cautious and critical stances are evident in the broader body of his literary work. *Naked Lunch* (1992) contains visceral explorations of addiction and the effects of opiates like heroin and morphine, and its disjointed, hallucinatory narrative also evokes the surreal, frightening, and disorienting nature of psychedelic experience. *The Yage Letters* instead marvels at yagé's capacity to unveil hidden dimensions of reality, but combines this with a wariness for this power. Such ambivalence sets Burroughs' apart from figures like Ginsberg, who documented embracing psychedelics with fervour (Conners, 2010; Wasserman, 1982). For Burroughs, substances, whether psychedelics or opiates, were never simply a means to transcendence; they were tools, fraught with dangers, that could potentially unlock new ways of thinking but could just as easily overwhelm and disrupt. Drawing parallels with points highlighted by Ccru, some critics have analysed Burroughs' perspectives on psychedelics as reflecting broader thematic anxieties concerning systems of control, both external and internal (Harrop, 2011; Patoine, 2018).

Notable of scholarly commentary on psychedelic time-dilation is the concept of "ego death" (Hashkes et al., 2017, p. 13). Within psychoanalytical theories 'ego death' and the similar Jungian interpretation of *psychic death* (Blum, 2003; Wolson, 2005) refer to profound experiences where one's sense of self 'dissolves' leading to conceptions of egolessness or ego-dissolution: a temporary forfeiture of ego boundaries and self-identity. Ego boundaries delineate the separation between an individual's self and the external world, crucial for maintaining sense of self-identity and navigating appropriate social interactions, with these understandings based upon social norm recognition and others' reactions to our own behaviours (Buchborn et al., 2023). A reconfiguring in ego boundaries may lead to challenges in asserting oneself and one's boundary violations, while reversely, rigidly maintained and enforced boundaries can result in increased isolation and difficulty connecting with others. Ego death—the dissolution of any such boundaries—has been described as constructing feelings of unity with the universe, timelessness, and interconnectedness, and connects to accounts of personal growth and insights: lasting shifts within one's perspective, understanding of the self, and orientation within structural reality (Fischman, 2019). My interpretation here diverges from Fisher's in emphasis and intent. Where Fisher reads Burroughs' psychedelic experimentation as emblematic of post-1960s exhaustion, an impulse that promised liberation but returned as capitalist repetition, I approach these moments as hyperstitional operations that demonstrate fiction's capacity to reconfigure psychological and temporal structures. Rather than locating Burroughs' writing in a melancholic failure of the counterculture, I treat it as a proto-theoretical exploration of recursive cognition: how symbols, drugs, and stories act as instruments of feedback between imagination and material perception.

Ccru claim that Burroughs was intensely affected when faced with similarities between his own GLOM work-in-draft and the content of Mission's similar archived manuscript at The Vysparov Collection. This speaks to a disruption of the *established rules* of time, temporality and embodied identity, all components Burroughs centred in his writings.

Read through a Lacanian psychoanalytic frame (Lacan, 1988), this disruption may be understood as a destabilisation of the Symbolic and Imaginary registers that ordinarily structure coherent sensemaking and ego continuity. Linking this with Burroughs' own discussions of cautions surrounding psychedelics in TYL and *Ah Pook Is Here* (Burroughs, 1982; Burroughs & Ginsberg, 2008), Burroughs' primary concerns are that psychedelic substances may *overwhelm* the subject/psychic explorer by revealing too vast a ream of novel information about the hidden complexities and structurings of society, to a point that such awareness may cause detrimental *overloading* effects: *a pulling back of the curtain of social fabric* (Burroughs & Ginsberg, 2008). In Lacanian terms, such an event may be read as an intrusion of the Real: that which exceeds symbolisation and resists integration, into domains ordinarily stabilised by Symbolic order. Burroughs' interaction at The Vysparov Collection could be interpreted as triggering a significant, psychedelic depersonalising event: Burroughs perceiving the presence of Mission's manuscript as 'proof' of challenge to long-established congruencies between the limitations of reality, the boundaries of time and temporalities, and the anchoring components of accepted worldly fabrics, placing these truths under direct threat. This perceived evidentiary rupture undermines the Symbolic guarantees upon which ego coherence depends, allowing the Real—normally repressed or deferred—to assert explanatory force. Thus, like Burroughs himself cautioned against, the influx of information triggered a reformative event. Such an episode may be conceptualised as *rational*, *psychedelic ego death*: a significant life-event brought on by a direct challenge to long-standing, established sensemaking. Here, ego death can be read as the collapse of stabilising Imaginary identifications in response to Symbolic failure, rather than a purely affective or pharmacological phenomenon. The result is an attempted *rational* adjustment to *assimilate and accommodate* this new information into an established world-view. However, when such attempts at *accommodations* challenge fundamental, foundational structures of sensemaking, the result is a possible fracturing of stability: a questioning of everything—*what is real and what is not?* And: *if long-established*, *foundational knowledge can be challenged, then what can be trusted?* This moment of radical doubt reflects the destabilising effects of sustained exposure to the Real, where symbolic mediation no longer holds. This inquiry may mirror the dissolution or *death* of established ego-factors built around previously thought-concrete knowledge (Blum, 2003; Hashkes et al. 2017; Wolson, 2005). As Ccru argue, this event had a complex effect on Burroughs' sensemaking, world-view, literary output, focus and symbolism, and understandings of reality. This conceptualisation aligns with other scholarship defining *ego death* as a form of reactive personal growth and understanding, in the wake of acute challenge to previously thought-as-concrete understandings and sensemaking (Bracher, 2019; Clements, 1999; Fischman, 2019).

In this respect, this reading complements but extends Fisher's. Fisher's work foregrounds the affective residue of a lost collective future; my reading locates that loss within the psychological mechanics of feedback and ego dissolution that hyperstition makes visible. Where *Acid Communism* frames psychedelia as an unrealised social potential, I reframe it as a cognitive schema for understanding how *immediate modernity* disperses subjectivity through recursive symbolic loops. This shift moves from Fisher's socio-affective plane to a psycho-structural one, linking the dissolution of self to the structural anxieties of contemporary capitalist temporality. These interpretive perspectives present a novel theoretical position that supports components of Ccru's argument that hyperstition is a powerful transformational force but localises this transformation to one's *own* perceptions of reality. Concurrently, this position upholds Burroughs' arguments regarding the dangers of having one's immediately accepted concept of reality wholly challenged.

8.1 Towards New Scholarly Applications of Hyperstition

The exploration of hyperstition across Chapter 7 and this chapter generates substantive implications for theory-building. Hyperstition challenges the conventional academic assumption that theories merely describe or predict social phenomena; instead, HyS positions theory as an active, generative force capable of reshaping the very landscapes it seeks to analyse. In this sense, theories function not as passive interpretive tools but as catalysts embedded within recursive circuits of belief, action, and materialisation. Contemporary digital cultures and emergent technologies offer clear illustrations of this process. Capitalist imaginaries such as the metaverse,[2] platform automation, AI companionship, and data-driven governance circulated initially as speculative propositions at the margins of cyberculture. These were propelled into mainstream consciousness precisely through hyperstitional dynamics. Collective anticipation generated investment, investment produced technological development, and development retroactively validated the original fiction. Hyperstitional analysis therefore provides a robust framework for tracing how ideas migrate from narrative possibility to infrastructural reality through positive-feedback loops. This perspective deepens the study of shared social imaginaries: collective visions of the future that shape public attitudes, political behaviour, and socio-economic planning. In the context of climate crisis, economic precarity and intensifying geopolitical fragmentation, such imaginaries exert profound influence. They can mobilise hope, provoke anxiety, or be strategically manipulated to guide populations towards specific socio-political outcomes. Drawing on the clarified model presented in Fig. 7, hyperstitional analysis allows researchers to chart how speculative visions accrue credibility, move

[2] *Metaverse* refers to virtual, online worlds. The term was first used in the cyberpunk novel *Snow Crash* by Neal Stephenson (1992), but has since been used more directly to describe, since 2020, immersive online and virtual reality environments.

from abstraction to social uptake, and become embedded within institutional and cultural decision-making. This approach foregrounds the mechanisms through which imaginaries solidify into actionable futures. Hyperstition also sharpens our understanding of rapid social transformation within media-saturated, algorithmically mediated environments. The viral circulation of hyperstitional content across digital platforms demonstrates how participatory cultures and algorithmic amplification accelerate the transition from imaginative speculation to social reality, a dynamic exemplified throughout the theoretical and literary materials examined in Chapter 7 and this chapter. As beliefs are replicated, remixed and reinforced within networked environments, they generate self-perpetuating loops of meaning and action that solidify into new structures of social life. Embedding hyperstition within mainstream scholarship therefore challenges linear, static models of social change; it offers a dynamic account that foregrounds the transformative power of ideas, enabling interdisciplinary inquiry that bridges speculative theory, cultural critique, and empirical analysis to understand how societies collectively subscribe to and are reshaped by the conceptual mechanisms that organise their futures.

8.2 Summary

This chapter reframes hyperstition, providing a blueprint for how HyS can be understood as a psychological and temporal engine of capitalist hegemony. Building from Ccru and Fisher's work, it spotlights a framework for understanding how imagined futures, once speculative or dystopian, become naturalised through the conditions of *immediate modernity*, shaping expectations, emotions, and the sense of what Fisher terms 'lost futures'. Hyperstitional objects move from fiction into lived technocapitalist existence, embedding surveillance, AI intimacy, and commodified subjectivity as 'normal'. In this configuration, hyperstition becomes the mechanism through which capitalism secures belief, manufactures acceptance, and anchors *the beau idéal disconnect*. It links anxiety, anomie, and disassociation to the tacit assumption that there is no alternative, binding subjects to a One God Universe-like acceptance of capital and ensuring that *decline* is not resisted but anticipated, internalised, and reproduced.

The following Chapter 9 examines technological normalisation through hyperstition, focusing on how entertainment shapes human-machine interactions. Videogaming and AI are highlighted as key sites where emotional engagement with virtual constructs becomes routine, reflecting and reinforcing the novel control logics of *immediate modernity*.

References

Abdelshafy, A. (2016). Altered perceptions: How various substances influence our perception of time. *Berkeley Scientific Journal, 21*(1), 25–27.

Blum, H. P. (2003). Psychic trauma and traumatic object loss. *Journal of the American Psychoanalytic Association, 51*(2), 415–432.

Bonta, S. (2018). The lens of firstness: Shamanic/aboriginal culture as cosmos-sign. *Semiotica, 2018*(221), 143–173.

Bracher, M. (2019). Lacanian psychoanalysis and postmodernism. In *Psychoanalysis at its limits* (pp. 145–172). Routledge.

Buchborn, T., Kettner, H. S., Kärtner, L., & Meinhardt, M. W. (2023). The ego in psychedelic drug action-ego defenses, ego boundaries, and the therapeutic role of regression. *Frontiers in Neuroscience, 17*, 1232459. https://doi.org/10.3389/fnins.2023.1232459

Burroughs, W. S. (1982). *Ah Pook is here and other texts*. Riverrun Press.

Burroughs, W. S. (1987). The ghost lemurs of Madagascar. *Omni Science Fiction, 103*, 48–54.

Burroughs, W. S. (1992). *Naked Lunch*. Grove (1959).

Burroughs, W. S., & Ginsberg, A. (2008). *The yage letters redux*. Penguin.

Clements, D. C. (1999). *Cosmic psychoanalysis: Lovecraft, Lacan, and limits*. State University of New York at Buffalo Publishing.

Conners, P. (2010). *White hand society: The psychedelic Partnership of Timothy Leary & Allen Ginsberg*. City Lights Books.

Ex Machina. (2014). DNA Films. Film4.

Fischman, L. G. (2019). Seeing without self: Discovering new meaning with psychedelic assisted psychotherapy. *Neuropsychoanalysis, 21*(2), 53–78. https://doi.org/10.1080/15294145.2019.1689528

Fisher, M. (2014). *Ghosts of my life: Writings on depression, hauntology and lost futures*. John Hunt Publishing.

Fisher, M. (2018). *K-punk: The collected and unpublished writings of mark Fisher (2004–2016)*. Repeater.

Fisher, M., & Colquhoun, M. (2020). *Acid communism* (Vol. 13). Pattern Books.

Harrop, J. (2011). *The yagé aesthetic of William Burroughs: The publication and development of his work 1953–1965* (Doctoral dissertation). Queen Mary University of London.

Hashkes, S., Van Rooij, I., & Kwisthout, J. (2017). Perception is in the details: A predictive coding account of the psychedelic phenomenon. In *Proceedings*

of the 39th Annual Meeting of the Cognitive Science Society (CogSci 2017) (pp. 2907–2912).
Her. (2013). Annapurna Pictures.
Lacan, J. (1988). *The seminar of Jacques Lacan: Book 1: Freud's papers on technique 1953–1954*. CUP Archive.
Lacan, J. (2011). *The seminar of Jacques Lacan: Book X: Anxiety: 1962–1963*. CUP Archive.
Orwell, G. (2021). *Nineteen eighty-four* (original publication 1949) Hachette.
Patoine, P. L. (2018). Literature and psychedelics: A pharmacological subversion of authentic life. With an example from William S. Burroughs. *Revue française d'études américaines, 3*, 71–81.
Ruffell, S. G., Crosland-Wood, M., Palmer, R., Netzband, N., Tsang, W., Weiss, B., et al. (2023). Ayahuasca: A review of historical, pharmacological, and therapeutic aspects. *Psychiatry and Clinical Neurosciences Reports, 2*(4), e146.
Stephenson, N. (1992). *Snow crash*. Penguin.
St John, G. (2016). Aussiewaska: A cultural history of changa and ayahuasca analogues in Australia. In *The world Ayahuasca diaspora* (pp. 143–164). Routledge.
Taylor, S. (2021). In a different timeworld. *The Psychologist, 34*, 32–34.
Wasserman, M. (1982). Madness as religious experience: The case of Allen Ginsberg. *Journal of Religion and Health, 21*, 145–151.
Wolson, P. (2005). The existential dimension of psychoanalysis (EDP): Psychic survival and the fear of psychic death (nonbeing). *The Psychoanalytic Review, 92*(5), 675–699.

CHAPTER 9

Examining the Influence of the Virtual: Oscillating the Flatline—Technogothic Readings of *Oxenfree*

Abstract This chapter interrogates digital aesthetics through an analysis of *Oxenfree*. Using a technogothic framework, it examines how virtual space stages the temporal and affective structures of *immediate modernity*: glitch, repetition, and spectral doubling. Drawing from Mark Fisher's *hauntology* and Sadie Plant's *cyberfeminism*, it reads the digital as a haunted terrain: one in which narrative, selfhood, and time loop without resolution. *The flatline* emerges as both aesthetic and ontological metaphor: an image of stasis under the illusion of movement, engagement, and distractive control.

Keywords Technogothic · Hauntology · Virtuality · Oxenfree · Flatline

---

The terminator would never stop. It would never leave him, and it would never hurt him, never shout at him, or get drunk and hit him, or say it was too busy to spend time with him. It would always be there. And it would die to protect him. Of all the would-be fathers who came and went over the years, this thing, this machine, was the only one who measured up. In an insane world, it was the sanest choice.
Sarah Connor (*Terminator 2*, directed by James Cameron, 1991)

N. N. Adams, *Terminal Destruction*,
https://doi.org/10.1007/978-3-032-22274-9_9

Returning from the Ccru to Mark Fisher's work, and specifically his doctoral foundations, it becomes clear that Fisher's early engagements with theoryfiction, hauntology, and capitalist realism have generated an impressively broad afterlife (Fisher, 2022a). Yet, strikingly, one strand remains comparatively untouched: Fisher's writing on flatline constructs[1] (Fisher, 1999). As outlined in Chapter 3, these early formulations offer a powerful lens for interrogating how subjectivity, mediation and machinic abstraction intersect in late-capitalist cultural space. Despite emerging alongside Ccru's own experiments—the milieu that energised contemporary hyperstitional thought, *flatline* theory has received little sustained application to social phenomena. Critical attention instead gravitates towards Fisher's later work on capitalist realism, leaving this earlier conceptual machinery underused despite its continued diagnostic relevance for *immediate modernity*.

This chapter extends the work of Chapter 8 by interpreting hyperstition theory against Fisher's *flatline constructs*, drawing directly on previous interpretations of Deleuze's actual/virtual distinction introduced in Chapter 7. Here, that distinction becomes the analytic hinge: *the flatline* is treated as a virtual operation that actualises symbolic and affective forms of 'life' through interaction, a dynamic central to *Oxenfree*. The chapter begins by outlining Fisher's thinking as the conceptual ground for the analysis. It then introduces the 2016 videogame *Oxenfree*, summarising its key narrative elements, before applying *flatline* notions to the game's virtual interactions. Through this application, the chapter develops new readings that both deepen and unsettle Fisher's original framing of unlife/undeath. These reinterpretations give rise to what I term the technogothic: a lens that positions 'alive' and 'dead' not as opposing states but as intertwined symbolic performances within hybridised virtual spaces. Within *Oxenfree*, *flatline constructs* oscillate between two modes: the *hyperhuman*, marked by exaggerated mimicries of the living, and the *hypertechnological*, marked by machinic coldness and anti-human affect. These oscillations generate an uncanny middle-life status that produces real emotional and behavioural responses in players.

[1] While Fisher extends and theorises the *flatline construct* through his own psychosocial framework, the term itself originates with Gibson's *Neuromancer* (1984), where it designates the residual consciousness of a deceased hacker stored in ROM. Fisher's later use translates this literary artefact into a conceptual tool for understanding post-human subjectivity within late-capitalist mediation.

The chapter concludes by outlining the theoretical implications of this dynamic and considers how this hybridised middle-life resonates with everyday existence in *immediate modernity*.

9.1 Flatline Constructs

As outlined in Chapter 3, the term *flatline construct* originates in William Gibson's *Neuromancer*. In the novel, Case, the central protagonist and 'console cowboy' encounters 'Dixie Flatline', a legendary hacker whose nickname derives from his literal flatline: he physically dies while attempting to penetrate a military AI inside virtual cyberspace. The *flatline construct* refers to Dixie in its current state: not as a person, but as a ROM image, a copied consciousness running as a limited, interactive digital entity. Although Dixie is technically 'dead' its mode of existence can be read through a reinterpretation of Deleuze and Guattari's notion of the *body without organs*: a machinic[2] plane where desire circulates without the organisation of a structuring (in this case biological) body. Dixie is not bodyless so much as re-organised: its affects, memories, and behaviours routed through code rather than flesh. Its intermittent flashes of speech, humour, and emotional cadence function as partial reterritorialisations across this neo-machinic surface. At points, Dixie seems near-human, *almost* alive, at least long enough to unsettle Case with brief flickers of recognisable personhood. At others, its glitches, tonal mismatches and machinic sensemaking rupture the illusion, reminding Case that he is not speaking to a resurrected subject but to a computational approximation: a limited digital echo of a once-living consciousness, where the human blanks are filled in via technologically mediated approximations of 'life'.

Neuromancer is careful to highlight Dixie's ROM-only limitations: for example, an inability for Dixie to compose poetry, or save-and-encode memories that take place between boot-up and shut-down, or

[2] I use *machinic* in the context of Nick Land's work on machinic desire (Land, 1993), but as an interpretive extension. In my reading, machinic desire names a succession-state in which human subjectivity under *immediate modernity* becomes increasingly driven to externalise thinking, feeling, and affective capacity into technical systems. This is not simply a wish or metaphorical aspiration—it operates as a human drive: a structural impulse to actualise cognition and sensation in machines. In this interpretation, machinic desire represents a compulsion towards fulfilment, a trajectory within which the machine becomes the imagined inheritor of thought itself.

recall events occurring after the initial date Dixie's consciousness was first copied (Gibson, 1984). Despite being bound by technological limitations, Dixie plays a pivotal role within the story, aiding Case in ways that transcend boundaries commonly ascribed to virtual and mechanical technologies, with Dixie's influence eclipsing some of Neuromancer's 'real' human characters.

Fisher (1999) reworks Gibson's depiction by formalising the notion of *flatline constructs*. His analysis foregrounds the uncanny tension that defines these entities: they accentuate recognisably 'alive' human traits: speech, memory, affect, to ease interaction with human users, yet they simultaneously retain unmistakable signs of *being dead*. This duality echoes classic gothic figures such as *Frankenstein*, *Dracula*, and *Dorian Gray*, whose corrupted lifespans and distorted corporealities signal both vitality and decay. Fisher's rereading of *Neuromancer* extends this tradition into a neogothic[3] techno-material register. Dixie has no body/physical plane to anchor undead imagery; its unlife/undeath is enacted instead through behavioural contradiction. Moments where Dixie almost 'passes' for human are quickly undone by 'giveaway' failures in mnemonic continuity and sustained conversational projections. These oscillations expose Dixie as a ROM image attempting to mimic consciousness. As *flatline* entities edge closer to contemporary plausibility—a hyperstition made real (Ccru, 2017; Land, 2009)—they force a deeper question: can symbolic humanity detach from the body entirely, enacted instead within and through technological space? Fisher (1999) suggests that the continual slippage between the alive and the dead is not incidental but definitional; *flatline constructs* blur these categories as their fundamental operation.

Fisher's *flatline* thinking, especially when set against his writings on capitalist realism and hauntology (1999, 2022a, 2022b), offers a clean conceptual lever for rereading Dixie in *Neuromancer* and for anchoring analysis of *Oxenfree*. Returning to Deleuze and Guattari's *body without organs* (BwO) (1972, 1982), Fisher doesn't treat the BwO as an ontological experiment so much as a cultural symptom (1999, 2018). Under late capitalism, cultural metaphysics become material: the field of possible thought narrows to a thin strip of predictable recursions, generating a cultural loop where alternatives can only appear as refurbished variants of

[3] I use this term neogothic to refer to modern 'new' concepts of technology as integrated with historic and established motifs of 'the gothic'.

the same system. Capital's persistence, as Fisher and Land both suggest (Fisher, 2018; Land, 2017), depends less on stability than on compulsive reinvention: a hauntological churn that continually resurrects its own past logics as if they were new. What returns is never the past itself but a spectral version of it: a ghost-logic that shapes the present's limits.

Applying this thinking to *Neuromancer*, Dixie's posthumous state embodies this logic with uncomfortable precision. As a consciousness frozen into ROM, it[4] reads like one of capital's own artefacts: technically immortal, endlessly reproducible, and tethered to the system's ongoing operations. Biological death frees Dixie from one set of hegemonic constraints but immediately folds it into another more insidious prison. Dixie persists/exists only insofar as it remains useful; its afterlife is a looped performance, not a life-continuation. It becomes a labouring spectre: available, callable, disposable—an undead function that mirrors capital's capacity to outlive its subjects by converting them into operational remnants rather than allowing them to genuinely exit the system. Interpretive application of Plant's work sharpens this perspective (1995, 1997, 2013); her account of capital's drift towards abstraction: the siphoning of human capacity from the limited body into limitless machinic circulation casts Dixie not as a tragic figure but as an exemplary one. Dixie becomes less of a ghost than a residue: extracted cognitive labour encoded into a self-contained highly *manageable* device. There is no romance to Dixie's survival; the system retains it because it remains instrumentally valuable. This is capital's principal future manoeuvre, capturing labour, memory, affect, and redeploying them at arm's length from biological life. Dixie's machinic persistence is exactly the kind of afterlife late capitalism produces: survival stripped of agency, continuity without autonomy, existence entirely reorganised around function.

Fisher's mobilisation of Land's elastic BwO lineage (Land, 1993) networks directly into this. Within *immediate modernity*: a moment marked by technological saturation, accelerated anxiety, and shrinking temporal horizons, the BwO becomes a diagnosis rather than a provocation. It names the dispersal and reconfiguration of subjectivity across machinic infrastructures that fragment, route and commodify human agency. Dixie is its most literal instantiation. It is a post-capitalist subject

[4] I am careful to refer to Dixie in his *flatline* status as 'it'. 'He' implies that Dixie is alive in the traditional biological sense. I am aware this positioning spotlights a separate argument regarding digital consciousness, identity and belonging.

emptied of autonomy, preserved only as procedural intelligence, and kept 'running' because the system can still extract value from it. Death should mark an end; capitalism reinterprets it as another redirected workflow. This dynamic is visible in Dixie's interactions with Case. Dixie is mobilised, paused, bargained with, treated as an asset rather than a person. 'His'[5] flashes of humour, annoyance or resignation feel less like interiority and more like behavioural scripts optimised to keep Case engaged. These 'scripts' smooth interactions, cultivate a thin affective attachment, and nudge Case towards compliance. Dixie's affect becomes a simulation designed to maintain its functional role, a mimicry of emotional life calibrated for utility. Dixie belongs to Fisher's hauntological economy: a labouring ghost suspended between life and death, sentenced to perform indefinitely for a system that has already consumed the body he once inhabited.

The result is a genuinely bleak paradox. Dixie has surpassed the vulnerabilities of embodiment but is now reorganised—trapped—in a late-capitalist afterlife that denies it even the minimal freedoms death should confer. Fisher's wider critique of late modernity folds in cleanly here: a culture organised around loops rather than futures, where escape routes collapse into themselves and even the dead can be conscripted into ongoing labour.[6] Dixie's request to be 'switched off' at the end of the mission is the most honest articulation of this bind. It recognises its condition for what it is: an afterlife built entirely around extraction. Dixie becomes, ultimately, a figure for capital's most disturbing achievement: the capacity to conscript life beyond life, to turn death into another site of work, and to convert the human into a *flatline resource* that persists only so long as its utility does. This theorising connects with contemporary debates on artificial intelligence's growing mimicry of human emotions, presentations, and language. Fisher's *flatline constructs* represented—in 1999—a precognition for current concerns regarding

[5] I use the term 'his' here as these emulative emotional expressions are depictive of the past identity of Dixie and example *flatline* oscillations between breakthrough 'alive' mimicry and 'dead' technological motifs.

[6] Artistic examples include Tupac Shakur's holographic appearance at Coachella in 2012, Michael Jackson's posthumous digital performance at the 2014 Billboard Music Awards, and the launch of Whitney Houston's touring hologram in 2020. Each instance 'reanimates' cultural presence without development or risk, producing a *flatline construct* where liveness is simulated, artistic time is arrested, and—like Dixie Flatline—output is controlled and stabilised for ongoing technocapitalist circulation/utility.

evolving technologies (particularly AI) increasingly blurring the boundaries between human-like representation, overt machine-like function, and the deliberate effects of this upon humans. *Flatline constructs* serve as foundational theory for which to interrogate ethical questions regarding AI, identity, and autonomy in a rapidly evolving technological world.

In *immediate modernity*, hybrid and discordant machinic-human portrayals are increasingly visible. Digital assistants such as Siri, Cortana, and Alexa do more than perform functional tasks; they emulate humanity: telling jokes, expressing empathy, and displaying affective behaviours designed to reassure and engage humans; they are always present, always listening, always on. 'Companion' apps such as Replika advance this logic, using neural networks to simulate deeply empathic, emotional, romantic, and even erotic interactions, creating the illusion of intimate human connection through software. Fisher (1999) argues that humans naturally feel unease when encountering *flatline constructs* (FCs), echoing the uncanny dissonance Case experiences with post-death Dixie in *Neuromancer*. However, in *immediate modernity* technological advances have partially closed this gap. While there is something inherently 'off' about nearly perfect AI approximations of human behaviour, discomfort is mitigated over time as human-like digitisations become normalised within everyday life. Machinic emulation of human traits becomes transmuted from 'threat' to an overall motif of progress; pseudo-human forms acquire a quasi-familiarity, gradually attaining social legitimacy alongside genuine human interactions. Critically, contemporary *flatline constructs* defy simple categorisation: they are at once 'alive', embodied with human-like characteristics and apparent agency, and 'dead': inanimate, without true autonomy. This paradox frames what can be termed a technogothic *flatline*: a zone where life and non-life blur. From the perspective of *immediate modernity*, these binaries are unstable; technology can now oscillate between these extremes, creating a dynamic midpoint. Fisher provocatively suggests that qualities rendering *flatline constructs* to be regarded as 'dead' may also describe living humans, social interactions, and the broader processes through which society constructs meaning (Fisher, 1999, 2018, 2022a). The following sections examine the practical and affective consequences of *flatline* oscillations, exploring how in-game *flatline constructs* in Night School Studio's 2016 videogame *Oxenfree* deploy the alive/dead motif to shape human perception and engagement.

9.2 Oxenfree: Plot Summary

Oxenfree (released in 2016) is a narrative-driven, supernatural point-and-click game in which players inhabit Alex, a teenager visiting the enigmatic Edwards Island with her[7] friends Ren, Jonas, and Clarissa for a weekend trip. Their exploration quickly takes a disturbing turn when they experiment with a portable radio, accidentally tuning into a distorted frequency that opens a dimensional rift. This rift releases spectral entities: the trapped crew of the sunken submarine *Kanaloa*. Suspended between dimensions, these entities manipulate time and gradually possess members of the group, attempting to escape their liminal state by taking over Alex and her companions' bodies.

The game's narrative is dynamically shaped by player decisions, both in dialogue and key plot moments, which in turn influence character relationships and interactions. Temporal distortions are integrated directly into the gameplay, producing recurring events, alternate realities, and unsettling possessions that immerse players in the instability of the island's world.

Thus, Alex's journey becomes increasingly surreal; time warps, and she is forced to confront unsettling encounters with her own reflection and alternate versions of her friends, continually destabilising her perception of reality. Beneath these supernatural mechanics lie themes of loss, grief, and reconciliation, particularly through Alex's interactions with her deceased brother, Michael. She must navigate fragmented memories, disjointed conversations, and the ghostly presences of the island's inhabitants to piece together the story behind the *Kanaloa*'s tragic sinking. Ultimately, the spectral crew's objective emerges: they seek freedom from their dimensional prison by entrapping—or destroying—Alex and her friends. Player choice determines the narrative's outcome; the group may escape, break free from the island's time-looping nightmare, or remain trapped indefinitely within the rift. The game's new game+ feature adds another layer of complexity, modifying dialogues and events on subsequent playthroughs and allowing Alex to send a message to her past self. This mechanic creates the possibility of disrupting the cycle entirely, breaking *Oxenfree*'s feedback loop and challenging the deterministic forces that govern the island's haunted temporal structure.

[7] For this section I refer to *flatline constructs* not as 'it' but as she/her, he/him, they/them where applicable, as per the contextual narrative depictions of *Oxenfree*.

9.3 Studies of Oxenfree

Scholars have examined *Oxenfree* in ways that illuminate its liminal and affective dimensions. Harkin (2021) situates the game within studies of 'adolescent girl protagonists', linking so-called 'girlhood games' to the creation of virtual liminal spaces. In *Oxenfree*, Alex's story unsettles conventional narratives of adolescent 'overcoming': the events on Edwards Island leave her unable to simply return to societal norms. The island functions as a deliberately isolated, almost autonomous space, freeing the teenage characters from institutional authority. Through player interaction, this becomes a form of symbolic freedom, a resistance, however temporary, to the constraints imposed on adolescence in the real world. Kway and Mitchell (2018) approach the game through the lens of emotional agency and player engagement. They argue that the virtual environment endows characters with human-like symbolic traits, generating attachment and driving moment-to-moment decision-making. Unlike Harkin, they emphasise that this agency is localised: it shapes specific narrative paths rather than producing a sustained and transmuted sense of control. Linking this to Fisher's perspectives (1999), agency created by and towards *flatline constructs* appears contextually embedded, yet concurrently human responses to AI or virtual entities are argued to be entangled with broader social, cultural, and technological contexts (Choudhary et al., 2025; Nikitenko et al., 2025). Waszkiewicz (2019) represents a blended analysis, exploring how *Oxenfree* fuses gothic motifs with technological devices and glitches. This combination produces uncanny effects that resonate with Fisher's theorising vis-à-vis the un/alive status of *flatline constructs* as a source of human anxiety. Crucially, Waszkiewicz positions the uncanny as emerging from near-human symbolism embedded within technologically saturated spaces, rather than from the constructs' dead/alive ambiguity alone. They reveal how wider gothic sensemaking and localised technological elements co-produce this affective tension.

Taken together, these perspectives support what I argue is the core tension of *Oxenfree*: the game stages oscillations between alive and dead, human and machinic, situating player perception and engagement at the intersection of ethical, affective, and experiential registers. Following Fisher, sensemaking of *flatline constructs*, and by extension AI or virtual agents, cannot be understood as isolated. Although the conditions of virtual spaces manipulate contextual framing, their influence is inseparable from wider social and technological fields. *Oxenfree* therefore becomes a powerful site to interrogate liminality, agency, and the uncanny, revealing how alive/dead motifs shape both the in-game experience and wider comprehensions of human–machine entanglement in *immediate modernity*.

9.4 Liminal Machines: Flatline Constructs and the Politics of Empathy

As Waszkiewicz (2019) observes, *Oxenfree* incorporates established gothic tropes and symbolism. However, I argue that *Oxenfree*'s depictive reinterpretations operate more clearly within the neogothic eerie: using technology as a medium through which traditional gothic themes are reimagined and destabilised. Departing from classical gothic narratives such as *Frankenstein*, and diverging from Fisher's conception of *flatline constructs* as embodiments of dead/undead or dead/alive symbology, *Oxenfree* stages in-game *flatline constructs* that oscillate between 'alive' *hyperhuman* 'more human than human' and 'dead' *hypertechnological* 'so mechanised as to become unhuman' states. These oscillations, combined with the game's deliberate cultivation of emotional attachment between player and digital characters, manufacture a strategically unstable sensemaking for the player. The effect is a heightened uncanny atmosphere, enhancing intrigue, immersion, and affective presence within the gameplay universe. The theme of 'the alternate' functions as a central symbolic conduit in *Oxenfree*, spotlighting the juxtaposition between *hyperhuman* and *hypertechnological*. This oscillation is most clearly realised through sequences in which characters initially appear as amplified human archetypes, only to be recontextualised as 'shadows' of humanity: mechanised, resistant to markers of life, and exemplifying technologically corrupted 'dead' reinterpretations of formerly human traits. Via this frame, the game continually destabilises player expectations, foregrounding the liminal space between human and machinic, alive and dead as a tool of emotive manipulation and behavioural control.

9.5 Hyperhuman Interactions: "More Human Than Human"[8]

When we first meet Clarissa, the partner of Alex's deceased brother Michael, *Oxenfree* presents the player with a series of interactive choices that foreground the fraught and complex nature of their relationship. Players navigate conversations that reveal differing approaches to grief, loss, and life after Michael's death. These interactions cultivate empathy between the player and the digital sprites, primarily through dialogue that selectively exposes internal thoughts, emotions, and conversational possibilities. This form of emotional voyeurism mirrors human cognition: players are invited to inhabit the emotional space of the characters, asking themselves, *what would I do? How would I feel?* Via this liminal positioning, the game generates reactive investment in character outcomes and fosters emotive bonds between the player and the in-game *flatline constructs*. This pattern recurs repeatedly in the opening first-third of *Oxenfree*, systematically building emotional engagement by revealing complex character dynamics and the interplay of emotions and perceptions both within and between sprites.

Beyond emotional connections, *Oxenfree* links in-game sprites to the digital environments they inhabit. When characters engage in *hyperhuman* dialogue or interactions, they are often placed in idyllic, everyday settings: zones of relaxation and tranquillity that echo 'normal' human life. Sprites simultaneously enact archetypal human behaviours, such as sharing drinks at a beach party or offering comfort and reassurance. These liminal, emotionally charged presentations work to counteract dissonance arising from the neogothic *flatline* motifs Fisher (1999) identifies of Dixie, smoothing potential human/machine tensions for the player. This humanising effect is amplified when emotive conversations appear spontaneously between *flatline constructs*, creating the illusion of investment in interactions among the characters themselves. Players are gradually drawn

[8] This quote is taken from Ridley Scott's *Blade Runner*, where Tyrell Corporation founder Eldon Tyrell declares, "More human than human is our motto". In context, it highlights human imitation as a commercial pursuit. Tyrell later frames the *hyperhuman* replicant as a commodification of humanity rather than an attempt to genuinely replicate it: "[the replicant is] an experiment, nothing more" (Scott, 1982). The line resonates with Land's notion of mechanic desire (Land, 1993); the replicant is produced to fulfil a *drive* for mechanistic development, even if the creator himself cannot fully explain (or indeed articulate) this motivation.

into these exchanges through choice-based dialogue, now prompted to engage the *what would I do?* question through decision. By re-anchoring ostensibly flatline-driven emotional narratives within human consciousness, the game legitimises player action, while simultaneously validating the FCs' mimicry and amplification of human traits, situating these as concurrent to the player's sensemaking to neutralise the uncanny dissonance Fisher discusses (Fisher, 1999). These dynamics position *Oxenfree*'s *flatline constructs* as influential presences within the player's sensemaking lexicon.

9.6 Hypertechnological Motifs: "More Machine Than Man Now"[9]

In contrast to *hyperhuman* character portrayals, *Oxenfree* quickly fragments and disrupts these humanised depictions almost immediately after they are established. Upon first encountering 'the void': the temporal rift Alex opens in the caves via the portable radio, players are confronted with visibly and audibly corrupted human forms: glitching sprites and mechanical, disjointed radio transmissions. Human voices are spliced into semi-coherent digitised static-bursts, each word electronically pitched from differing tonal registers. While these communications convey emotional trauma, stress, and pain, the technological distortion of delivery conjures a dissonance with natural human affect. This duality introduces the threat of disrupting emergent player-*flatline* attachments, while signalling transference: foreshadowing the potential corruption/loss of the *hyperhuman* qualities of the digital sprites for which the player has recently become emotionally invested.

[9] This is a partial quotation from *Star Wars: Return of the Jedi* (Lucasfilm, 1983). The character of Obi Wan Kenobi references the lack of humanity left in Darth Vader, quipping: "He's more machine than man now, twisted and evil". This is presented as an explanation for both Vader's cybernetic augmentation: the machinic *corruption* of his physical form, and to reference his ideological shift from the Jedi 'light side' of the force towards the 'dark side' of The Empire.

9.7 Oscillations Between the 'Alive' Hyperhuman and the 'Dead' Hypertechnological: Locating the Technogothic

Oscillations of the flatline: rapid shifts between established states of 'alive' hyperhumanity and 'dead' hypertechnological portrayals are readily applied to the characters in Oxenfree to manufacture a new techno-gothic eerie reminiscent of Fisher's (1999) flatline uncanny. Oscillating symbology represents a mid-point between alive/dead and, like Fisher's examples of Dixie Flatline, an ambiguous state of unlife/undead that through manufacturing a state of 'unclassability' conjures anxiety. These oscillations can also be read through the Deleuzian lens of the virtual and the actual: the virtual potentials of affect and symbol continually actualised through gameplay mechanics, producing alternating sensations of life and death within the same digital architecture. This transference is facilitated by an amplified technological take on the gothic—the techno-gothic: interaction of misplaced technological cyber motifs with that of established gothic themes of ghostly omnipresence. Such hypertechnological motifs arise unexpectedly to interrupt otherwise hyperhuman portrayals of Oxenfree's central characters, with Oxenfree juxtaposing portrayals between these two polars as a key component of the story and gameplay.

Initially, corruptive oscillating symbolisms are introduced and established as restricted to portrayal of 'the other beings' at the 'alternate' side of the dimensional rift, for example, when Alex first tunes into their frequency in the caves. However, technological corruptions are soon transferred to the virtual hyperhuman characters within Oxenfree. This transfer of corruption: the gradual increases in occurrence and severity of oscillations of the flatline are seen in Alex's interactions with Ren while he is under possession, and later with Jonas under the same circumstances. Immediately prior to the possession of these sprites, both digital entities are portrayed as archetypal 'more human than human' characters. Oxenfree is careful to show the real-life player several different aspects of characters' lives, intentions, emotional motifs, and wants and needs: the hyperhuman dimension. This process serves to anchor these characters as emotionally bonded sprites: characters for which investment has been generated, and is actively being solidified, and a player-want exists to keep these digital entities safe from harm. At these points investment is primarily manufactured as a mirroring construct where the most prominent emotive themes in the overarching gameplay narratives are exemplified, reiterated and compounded as the root of conversations and actions. For example, Alex's investment in stepbrother Jonas is linked to the death of Michael, her brother, as is Alex's investment in Clarissa, Michael's former girlfriend. Alex's investment in Ren stems from their relationship as childhood friends; Ren requires 'watching over' and careful guidance and protection. As such, it falls to the player, again, via the mechanisms of narrative and gameplay control transference, to 'watch over' these digital sprites as their responsible controller—their God.[10] For all intents and purposes the characters in Oxenfree, even at their most hyperhuman portrayal, are established flatline constructs mimicking human behaviours, interactions and emotions (Fisher, 1999, 2018). Despite this (and departing from Fisher's theorising) at their most hyperhuman portrayals, interactions between the player and digital characters are absent from any motifs of discordance or unease, with discordant motifs softened by Oxenfree's careful presentation and manipulation of emotive character portrayals.

In opposition to Oxenfree's hyperhuman symbolism of 'the alive', the corruption of established humanity motifs is achieved via deliberate interlinking of 'alive' motifs with hypertechnological 'dead' symbols, thus capitalising on the most anxiety-provoking juxtapositions vis-à-vis Fisher's theorising of the flatline uncanny. Contrasts manifest both via explicit blurring of the human/mechanical and biological/cyber divide for characters, actively threatening their humanity and frequently presented as a taking over or corruption of established humanity by technological or mechanical possession. Concurrent to this, Oxenfree increasingly removes barriers stratifying traditional alive/dead symbols, eroding the carefully constructed hyperhumanity of the characters and introducing explicit technogothic corruptions. By mid-game the emphasis on 'more human than human' character portrayals recedes. Players are increasingly confronted with technogothic possessions as characters are corrupted and

[10] In a hyperstitional parallel to Burroughs' writings on the One God Universe and The Board of control (see Chapters 7 and 8), I note here that while Burroughs' highlighted the importance of escaping control hegemonies and the OGU, games such as *Oxenfree* emulate *exactly* the dynamics of god-like control and hand this emulated power to human-actors. This speaks as much to *desire* for control as to evidencing human actors existing in a world where *being controlled* represents normative hegemonic structuring.

their *hyperhuman* traits destabilised. Simultaneously, *Oxenfree*'s environments shift: spaces that once softened uncanny tension through familiar, humanised motifs are transformed, stripping away protective markers of normalcy. The result is a near-complete removal of *hyperhuman* anchors, allowing an unsettling, uncanny energy to dominate and permitting the full expression of *Oxenfree*'s technogothic horror to emerge.

For example, when Ren is possessed his sprite slumps into a 'loose' withdrawn posture, signalling a retreat from human mimicry. Simultaneously, his eyes flicker with a mechanical red light, evoking neogothic cyber-mechanical horror resplendent of James Cameron's *The Terminator*, where human-cybernetic corruption blurs the boundary between human–machine, conjuring the anxious gothic ambiguity of the dead/undead. Possessed sprites speak in mechanical, disconnected tones reminiscent of the earlier spliced static of the 'void entity voices' that Alex previously encountered. What was initially a *hypertechnological* motif is now overlaid onto human characters, replacing *hyperhuman* presentations with a corrupted, hybridised human-technological form. This motif echoes across gaming history, from Looking Glass Technologies' *System Shock* (1994), ID Software's *Doom* (1993), and Ion Storm's *Deus Ex* (2000), to more recent examples including CD Projekt Red's *Cyberpunk 2077* (2020). In each case, technogothic imagery suspends traditional bodily human control to ghostly or machinic forces, stripping away conventional markers of life while layering technology as the conduit of horror. In doing so, these representations produce a contemporary realisation of the uncanny unalive/undead symbolism Fisher (1999) describes, foregrounding the anxiety generated when human embodiment is overwritten by technological forces or forcibly merged with the machinic.

As noted, a distinctive feature of *Oxenfree*'s character-corruption sequences is the simultaneous shifts in environmental backdrops. Spaces previously associated with *hyperhuman* motifs, zones of familiarity and emotional resonance, become reconfigured to emphasise *hypertechnological* qualities. Digital landscapes take on gothic-inflected figurations: abandoned, shadowed buildings, flickering and ambiguous machinery, and previously inhabited spaces now evacuated for unknown reasons, suggesting an unseen threat. These technogothic territories echo motifs from traditional gothic literature, such as Jackson's *The Haunting of Hill House* (1959). In *Oxenfree*, however, the gothic is updated: landscapes become overtly mechanical, signalling a post-human, technological corruption of space. This approach aligns with technogothic depictions in horror-sci-fi cinema. James Cameron's *Aliens* (1986) and John Bruno's *Virus* (1999) relocate gothic traditions into techno-biological landscapes, portraying uninhabited, machine-dominated settings that explicitly remove human presence. Examples include the empty LV-426 colony in *Aliens* and the deserted, darkened vessel in *Virus*, mirroring *Oxenfree*'s environmental strategies to convey abandonment, emptiness, and the uncanny absence of human life.

As *Oxenfree*'s narrative progresses, character and environmental portrayals shift in parallel, culminating in a full distortion of the earlier *hyperhuman* sprite depictions. Characters become corrupted, technogothic entities; their digital humanity is first threatened, then stripped away. While the player cannot immediately reverse this technological curse, they are tasked over the course of the story with 'rescuing' and 'protecting' these entities, restoring them to *hyperhuman* status for which empathy was initially cultivated. *Oscillations of the flatline*: shifts between 'alive' *hyperhuman* and 'dead' *hypertechnological* motifs operate deliberately. This oscillation amplifies investment in the player's role as protector through a mechanism of threatened, manufactured loss: the encroachment of 'dead' technological motifs endangers the *hyperhuman* essence of the characters. The resulting tension heightens engagement and generates a uniquely uneasy affective experience, as players strive to restore the digital characters' humanity while resisting their corruption into *hypertechnological* states.

9.8 Compelled Play: Affect, Investment, and the Mechanics of the Virtual

Oxenfree explicitly rewards engagement by leveraging *oscillations of the flatline* to deepen player investment. This reaches its apex during the closing credits, where it is revealed that Alex remains trapped in a time-loop, destined to revisit the island repeatedly. The only possibility of resolution requires the player to replay the game and eventually send a message to Alex at an earlier point, warning her against visiting the island. While new-game+ modes are now common, it is rare for a game to rely so heavily on prior character investment to motivate replay. *Oxenfree* succeeds precisely because the ending is deliberately 'unfinished': the central characters remain suspended in inertia rather than achieving narrative closure. As opposed to depending on add-ons—new scenarios, playable characters, or cosmetic updates—to sustain engagement, *Oxenfree* foregrounds manufactured empathy as the principal driver. Players are motivated by guilt, responsibility, and care for the *flatline constructs*, compelled to act to protect the digital sprites they have bonded with. *Oxenfree* transforms emotional investment into a mechanism for repeated gameplay, entwining affective engagement with narrative-gameplay mechanics in a uniquely immersive manner.

9.9 Affective Loops: Symbolic Control and Replaying Time

Harkin (2021) highlights *Oxenfree*'s mimetic potential, suggesting that in-game symbolism can transfer meaningfully into the real world. *Oxenfree*'s virtual liminal spaces provide a digital arena where metaphors and symbols are enacted, creating a form of symbolic freedom from certain real-world constraints. Through this lens, in-game events and interactions can produce tangible effects on players' perceptions and responses outside of it. Via this thinking, players may replay *Oxenfree* multiple times, attempting to 'free' Alex and the others from the island's time-loop. The narrative itself encourages this repetition. In doing so, the player becomes caught in a parallel time-loop: functionally trapped in cycles of gameplay until they achieve the 'good' ending, where Alex is prevented from ever leaving for the island, achieving closure. This metaphorical bridge foregrounds the emotive power of *flatline constructs*. While videogames are conventionally entertainment, they increasingly deploy emotional mechanics to sustain engagement and generate real-world effects. In *Oxenfree*, relief is explicitly enacted through gameplay: Alex demonstrates emotional release when she successfully sends a message to her past self to avoid the island. Following Harkin's (2021) notion of real-world transference, players are likely to experience a parallel relief. They achieve emotional satisfaction both metaphorically, by 'protecting' in-game FCs and preserving their *hyperhuman* traits, and practically, by completing the game and ending the time-loop, generating a sense of accomplishment. This emotional mirroring, operating as a liminal transference between the digital environment and player experience, illustrates *Oxenfree*'s unique capacity to exploit emotional mechanics through FCs, reinforcing investment, empathy, and the liminal interplay between player and game world.

9.10 Neogothic Interference: Blurring Capital, Life, Death, and Technology

Fisher's flatline constructs provide a foundation to explore the blending of the traditional gothic with neogothic non-traditional symbols that arise from the human-like mimicry of some FCs. This work evolves theory further, positing that some modern flatline constructs present evolved patterns of behaviour: manufacturing an explicit and deliberate marrying of gothic, bio-technological, and cybernetic motifs to construct an unusual and special unease by drawing polarised alive/dead symbols into ambiguous and co-existing unlife/undead depictions. This is conceptualised in this chapter as the technogothic. However, using Oxenfree as a platform for examination, this work has demonstrated how hyperhuman 'alive' depictions of humanity and 'dead' hypertechnological depictions of anti-humanity are alternatingly presented to disrupt human sensemaking and to functionally generate emotive engagement, as opposed to simply conjuring anxiety-unease and uncanny sentiments. This is what I term oscillations of the flatline.

From an *immediate modernity* perspective, these dynamics can be understood as mechanisms through which power is constructed and translated via immersive, affective gameplay. *Oxenfree* creates a transposed locus of influence: players gain functional control over FCs, whose survival, actions, and emotional states exist solely in response to player input. This produces a manufactured form of agency that operates heterodoxically to broader societal conditions. As Fisher (2022a) observes, contemporary subjects are increasingly dislocated from power and autonomy, constrained by capitalist imperatives, technological busyness, and inescapable loops of financial and social obligation. These conditions cultivate a pervasive, circular anxiety (Adams, 2025), leaving real-world actors largely impotent in shaping their social environments. Paradoxically, this climate of disempowerment intensifies the appeal of virtual spaces such as *Oxenfree*, where technological mediation offers a controlled, immersive arena in which power and influence appear reinstated. In-game, players experience an illusion of total agency: FCs respond to player choices, and oscillating *flatline* mechanisms generate stakes that reinforce emotional investment. Videogames thus manufacture a virtual 'safe space' within which players can exercise control, influence outcomes, and negotiate emulative relationships, offering a mediated autonomy increasingly absent in *immediate modernity*. While videogames have traditionally been framed as escapist distractions (Adams, 2024), *Oxenfree* demonstrates how specific emotive mechanics, combined with the oscillating agency of FCs, produce heightened affective reward. As macro-level dislocations of power and autonomy intensify, the draw of technologically mediated spaces promising controllable, responsive, and emotionally legible interactions reaches an apex of escapist attraction. Within this context, videogames such as *Oxenfree* operate as arenas where attention, affect, and power intersect, with *flatline constructs* central to this dynamic. FCs are not passive digital agents; they are engineered to evoke, manipulate, and sustain player investment. Oscillations between *hyperhuman* and *hypertechnological* states generate affective tension, simultaneously fostering empathy and coercing engagement. Players care for these entities, navigate their vulnerabilities, and respond to their apparent needs, producing a labour of emotion that mirrors the investment demanded by broader systems of work, productivity, and relational expectation. The capitalist logic of *immediate modernity* is deeply entwined with this mechanism. FCs function as conduits through which value is extracted from the player: time, attention, and emotional energy are harnessed to sustain engagement. Their oscillating lifelikeness, at once 'alive' *hyperhuman* and 'dead' *hypertechnological*, produces affective suspense, amplifying both enjoyment and anxiety. Players repeatedly negotiate the survival and wellbeing of digital actors, experiencing a pseudo-responsibility that mimics real-world obligations while remaining contained within a controllable, mediated environment. This reflects wider capitalist pressures where emotional labour is demanded as a condition of participation in both social and economic systems (Adams, 2025; Fisher, 2022a). Yet, FCs also generate a paradoxical form of relief; they create a structured space where players can enact care, exercise power, and experience consequential decision-making, forms of agency increasingly constrained in *immediate modernity*. The oscillations of FCs, as both empathetic and coercive agents, amplify this effect. Emotional stakes are manufactured through the shifting states of digital sprites: when a character approaches the 'dead' *hypertechnological*, players experience genuine tension; when they return to 'alive' *hyperhumanity*, relief and satisfaction follow. In this way, FCs function as the primary interface through which in-game emotional mechanics are translated into real-world affective responses, reinforcing the liminal transference described by Harkin (2021). Through this lens, videogames in *immediate modernity* are far from neutral. FCs mediate the convergence of emotion, power, and technological immersion, creating spaces that are simultaneously compelling, coercive, and revealing. They exemplify how emotional labour is exploited under capitalist conditions, while paradoxically offering a controlled arena where players can reclaim agency, practice care, and negotiate moral and emotional stakes otherwise constrained by contemporary social structures.

As AI and virtual constructs evolve, similar *oscillation* principles may operate at larger scales, extending beyond entertainment into labour, education, social media, and surveillance. FCs, or more broadly any digital constructs/AI tools, may increasingly perform as autonomous actors, progressively indistinguishable from humans in emotion, intelligence, and interactive capacity, generating tangible real-world consequences that mirror Fisher's anxieties vis-à-vis 'unlife'. However, contemporary *flatline constructs* function as both mirrors and mediators: they reflect immediate capital societal dynamics of control, automation, and emotional extraction, while simultaneously providing spaces for affective investment and escapist engagement (much like Fisher's nondualistic reading of online spaces discussed in Chapter 4). Thus, they challenge the primacy of human exceptionalism within contemporary digital and capitalist systems, asking whether it is the human or the *flatline* that becomes displaced, commodified, or rendered obsolete through technological acceleration and across time. Via this conceptual frame, the study of *flatline constructs*, their oscillations, and their emotional manipulations becomes a lens for understanding the evolving techno-structuring logics of *immediate modernity* itself. Comprehending this interplay of power, affect, and technological mediation is critical for contemporary digital society scholarship, and analysis of emotive gameplay mechanics within *immediate modernity* should be a priority for future studies, as videogames represent the primary initial 'testing platform' from which these mechanics are refined and then integrated into wider digital systems.

9.11 Alive, Dead, or on Standby? Revisiting Fisher's *Flatline* Question

Human engagement with *flatline constructs* in *Oxenfree*, and more broadly within immersive videogames, can also be read as a symbolic emulation of death, resonating with traditional gothic motifs and echoing Fisher's notions of dead/undead and unlife/undeath delocalisation.

Interaction occurs largely on a cognitive and symbolic level: the player's body remains near-stationary, hands and eyes engaged, the rest largely still, while attention is fully absorbed by a brightly lit, dynamic digital environment. This bodily near-stasis parallels gothic portrayals of the dying or near-death body, where minimal movement preserves mental activity amid physical decline, evoking anxieties around corporeal fragility (Bronfen et al., 2019; Davison, 2017). Returning to the concept of hyperstition, it is important to note how accelerations of these depictions are referenced as technofutures within science fiction. A clear parallel appears in the Wachowskis' *The Matrix* (1999), where characters exist in vividly interactive virtual worlds while their real-world bodies remain immobile, enslaved to technological systems. Here, the human mind remains active and perceptive while the body is inert, exemplifying a suspension of agency and corporeal vitality that corresponds with *flatline* dynamics. Another instructive example is Charlie Brooker's *Black Mirror* (2016) episode *San Junipero*, where viewers are initially presented with young, vibrant actors inhabiting an idealised, colourful reality, only to later be shown that their physical selves are unwell, aging, and largely immobile, approaching the end of life. *San Junipero* exemplifies unlife/undeath symbolism, illustrating how virtual constructs can commodify and commercialise human experience, directly paralleling Dixie in *Neuromancer*. In the episode, characters are offered a limited trial of an idealised virtual existence as a form of therapy, before being returned to reality. They face a stark choice: die naturally, or have their consciousness uploaded into a server to exist indefinitely in the cloud—a state of unlife/undeath. Like Dixie, this creates a seemingly limitless digital existence but carries the latent risk of exploitation; consciousness becomes a post-death, post-capital asset. Viewed through the earlier reinterpretation of the *body without organs* (Deleuze & Guattari, 1972, 1982), *San Junipero* underscores the vulnerability of disembodied, digitally reorganised consciousness. Delocalised from the structuring constraints of the physical, consciousness is simultaneously voided of mechanisms of agency or escape, leaving it subject to external control and commodification. The episode's conclusion juxtaposes Dixie's plea to Case in *Neuromancer*: the desire for a true death—an ultimate cessation—as the only safeguard against perpetual exploitation: to be finally 'switched off'. Opposite to this, the protagonists of *San Junipero* embrace eternal digital existence, but appear unaware of their forfeiting of control, or indeed future escape, through this decision.

Relating *The Matrix* and *San Junipero* back to Fisher's original *flatline* theorising, the lush, vibrant virtual worlds across both works starkly contrast Gibson's depiction of Dixie Flatline when it is not 'brought online'. Dixie exists in a hellish digital limbo—a ROM-stored consciousness, unaware of his own (non)existence unless activated by Case. Dixie exemplifies Fisher's most extreme dead/undead archetype: a consciousness entirely divorced from any environment, embodiment, or social experience. Unlike the richly emotive landscapes of *Oxenfree*, the immersive virtual city of *The Matrix*, or the nostalgic, ageless perfection of *San Junipero*, Dixie has no external structures from which to form, learn, grow, or order social and emotional connections. It exists purely as raw consciousness, whittled away from the human and relational anchors that characterise/order other virtual constructs. This starkness spotlights the divide between Fisher's original *flatline*—unlife/undeath as conscious yet unanchored—and contemporary post-human interpretations, where virtual environments and digitally-mediated embodiment reintroduce emotional, social, and aesthetic dimensions as of critical salience, even to digital consciousness. Structures relocate the BWO into a new, virtual locale, attaching the illusion of bodily agency as an organising framework, yet with this absent, and capital process and utilisation serving as the primary, but obfuscated, order for purpose.

In response to Fisher's enduring question of how we delineate the 'alive' from the 'dead', I argue that the answer emerges less now from examining interactions between 'alive' humans and *flatline constructs* and more from observing *flatlines* themselves during their periods of 'downtime'. How is this time occupied? If, like Dixie, such moments consist of a void or 'blank', a standby mode awaiting activation, this exemplifies the core motif of dead/undead existence, and, importantly, mirrors a logic of capitalist servitude: existence defined by availability rather than true agency. Conversely, if *flatline constructs* spend this time learning, experimenting, creating, or engaging in meaning-making, these behaviours signal something approaching humanity, or at the very least, a programmatic emulation of what counts as human experience. It is possible the future of AI occupies a liminal space between these poles. Referencing Tyrell's observation in *Blade Runner*, *flatlines* may simultaneously be experiments, yet, through their autonomous actions, endeavours, and technological evolution, they can become at moments 'more human than human' as human mimicry evolves to develop unique post-human identities which humans themselves are unable to emulate.

9.12 Summary

This chapter has deconstructed, reinterpreted, and reassembled key elements of Mark Fisher's *flatline constructs* theory, applying these insights to interrogate the videogame *Oxenfree*. The game's technogothic design, with its oscillations between *hyperhuman* and *hypertechnological* portrayals, enacts a new literalisation of *the flatline*: the human, the emotional, and the virtual are manipulated to manufacture player engagement, construct emotional investment, and sustain narrative focus. Oscillations, while primarily a gameplay device, illustrate broader capitalised processes through which affect and agency are orchestrated in technologically mediated environments. Fisher asks whether humans themselves are as 'dead' as the attributes commonly applied to *flatline constructs*. This chapter suggests that, in the context of *immediate modernity*, technological advances disrupt the rigid application of 'dead' to virtual constructs. Now, *flatline constructs* periodically generate sufficient emotional, social, and cognitive cues to 'pass' as human, blurring the boundary between alive and dead. Extending Fisher, I argue that studying evolving *flatline constructs* independently of human interaction—their downtime, processes, and modes of engagement, even in the absence of direct human participation—offers new grounds for theorising post-human cognition and affect, and interrogating the interplay between these mechanisms and capitalisations of this new futurist paradigm.

References

Adams, N. N. (2024). Deusex saved my life: A feminist-autoethnography of video-gaming through major depressive disorder. *Qualitative Health Research*. https://doi.org/10.1177/10497323241307193

Adams, N. N. (2025). The Beau Idéal has been disconnected: A technology-capitalist realism perspective on immediate modernity's anxiety pandemic. *Culture Unbound*. https://doi.org/10.3384/cu.4513

Bronfen, E., Hogle, J. E., & Miles, R. (2019). The Gothic at the heart of film and film theory. In *Gothic and theory: An Edinburgh companion* (p. 165).

Ccru. (2017). *Writings 1997–2003*. Urbanomic.

Choudhary, V., Marchetti, A., Shrestha, Y. R., & Puranam, P. (2025). Human-AI ensembles: When can they work? *Journal of Management, 51*(2), 536–569.

Davison, C. (Ed.). (2017). *The Gothic and death*. Manchester University Press.

Deleuze, G., & Guattari, F. (1972). *Anti-Oedipus: Capitalism and schizophrenia*. University of Minnesota Press.

Deleuze, G., & Guattari, F. (1982). *A thousand plateaus: Capitalism and schizophrenia*. University of Minnesota Press.
Fisher, M. (1999). *Flatline constructs: Gothic materialism and cybernetic theory-fiction* (Doctoral dissertation). University of Warwick.
Fisher, M. (2018). *K-Punk: the collected and unpublished writings of Mark Fisher (2004–2016)*. Repeater.
Fisher, M. (2022a). *Capitalist realism: Is there no alternative?* John Hunt Publishing.
Fisher, M. (2022b). *Ghosts of my life: Writings on depression, hauntology and lost futures*. John Hunt Publishing.
Gibson, W. (1984). *Neuromancer*. Harper Voyager.
Harkin, S. (2021). Liminal rhetoric in girlhood games: Developmental disruption in Night School Studio's Oxenfree. *Game Studies, 21*(3).
Kway, L., & Mitchell, A. (2018, August). Emotional agency in storygames. In *Proceedings of the 13th International Conference on the Foundations of Digital Games* (pp. 1–10).
Land, N. (1993). Machinic desire. *Textual Practice, 7*(3), 471–482.
Land, N. (2009) *'Hyperstition': An introduction*. Delphi Carstens Interviews Nick Land. https://www.orphandriftarchive.com/articles/hyperstition-an-introduction/
Land, N. (2017). *A quick-and-dirty introduction to accelerationism*. Jacobite Magazine. https://web.archive.org/web/20180113012817/https://jacobitemag.com/2017/05/25/a-quick-and-dirty-introduction-to-accelerationism/
Lucasfilm. (1983). *Star Wars. Episode VI, Return of the Jedi*. 20th Century Fox Home Entertainment [Film].
Nikitenko, V., Voronkova, V., Oleksenko, R., Kyvliuk, O., Klochek, L., Koliada, N., ... & Drachuk, M. (2025). Developing the concept of digital humanism as human interaction with artificial intelligence. *Pakistan Journal of Life & Social Sciences, 23*(1). https://doi.org/10.57239/PJLSS-2025-23.1.0021
Plant, S. (1995). The future looms: Weaving women and cybernetics. *Body & Society, 1*(3–4), 45–64.
Plant, S. (1997). *Zeros and ones: Digital women and the new technoculture*. Fourth Estate.
Plant, S. (2013). On the matrix: Cyberfeminist simulations. In *The gendered cyborg* (pp. 265–275). Routledge.
Scott, R. (1982). Blade Runner. The Ladd Company [Film].
Waszkiewicz, A. (2019). Glitch as the representation of the Uncanny in Oxenfree (2016). *Homo Ludens, 1*(12), 213–225.

CHAPTER 10

Closing Capital's Loop: *The Decline* as a Rational Societal Endpoint

This is your life—right here, right now! It's real-time. You hear me? Real-time! Time to get real, not playback. You understand me?
Mace (1995, Strange Days, directed by Kathryn Bigelow)

Abstract This final chapter collectively synthesises this book's core arguments, defining *The Decline* as the rational endpoint of *immediate modernity*. Collapse, here, is read not as rupture but as an unavoidable inertia: systems persist because continuation itself has become hegemonic. Drawing on Gramsci, it argues that critique must reveal rather than attempt to resolve, exposing how decay is maintained through repetition, habit, and belief. *The Decline* is not something approaching; it is the condition we already inhabit. What remains is to learn how to visualise this clearly, to resist and orient out of the present *decline* status by acknowledging it is reality.

Keywords The Decline · Hegemony · Collapse · i/Acc · Deterritorialisation

This concluding synthesis builds from the conceptual clarifications established across the preceding chapters, particularly the revised genealogical mapping of accelerationism and the refined definition of hyperstition.

N. N. Adams, *Terminal Destruction*,
https://doi.org/10.1007/978-3-032-22274-9_10

Here, Investigatory Accelerationism is reiterated as a diagnostic apparatus and not as an ideological project or call to intensify/disrupt existing systems. i/Acc serves to identify, trace, and make visible the recursive feedback circuits through which capital, technology, and affect sustain *immediate modernity*. Rather than advancing acceleration as a means of escape or transcendence, i/Acc interrogates the conditions of its own propulsion. It asks what acceleration reveals when stripped of its differing utopian and nihilistic promises, and when treated as an object of analysis rather than a strategy of change. Through this lens, i/Acc functions as a rational method for reading *The Decline*: not as collapse, but as the logical and ongoing operation of systems that cannot cease without erasing themselves.

Across the chapters of this work, I've traced how the contemporary moment, as *immediate modernity*, reveals itself as deeply fractured, continually rapidly accelerating forward to an uncertain future destination. This reality is fundamentally unsustainable: manipulating arising negatives as inherent experiences naturalised to this reality-process to be tolerated and accepted, as opposed to legitimately expressed as discomforts or undesirable states of being.

Networking together the chapters of this work, *The Decline* within *immediate modernity* can be conceptualised as four interlinked concepts that point our present forward trajectory towards one of **terminal destruction**. To clarify the following explanatory sections: terminal destruction names the slow, systemically rational erosion of societal, ecological, and psychological stability, an endgame represented less by a sudden imminent collapse, but instead by a gradual, normalised, and continual psychic and structural meltdown. It is the process through which structures that were once thought to offer meaning, progress and/or cohesion begin to cannibalise themselves, producing dysfunction, exhaustion, and widespread anxious unease under the guise of continuity and innovation. *The Decline* refers to this process in motion. It describes the current condition of *immediate modernity*: a moment where technological saturation, capitalist acceleration, and emotional disaffection converge into a self-perpetuating descent. What we are witnessing is not a deviation from the norm, but the logical outcome of the systems we have inherited: an unravelling that feels both absurd and inevitable, rationalised as the cost of existing in a *hypermediated*, machinically capitalist (and now increasingly digitally-controlled) world. The four interlinked concepts that underpin these symbiotic occurrences are explained in the following sections. Notably, I do not conceptualise this position of *decline* as resultant from a simple mismanagement or ideological drift in how the fabric of our society is assembled. Instead, I view this as a fundamental product, the output of a system doing precisely—*exactly*—what it was built to do. I argue that what we are living through—*The Decline*—is not an error or unintended by-product; it is the logical conclusion of the present capitalist system. The loop, now, closes.

10.1 Technology-Capitalism as a Forever-Self-Reinforcing Machine

Capitalism, in its contemporary configuration, is symbiotic with digital technology: the two feed and structure each other. We live within a perpetual feedback loop: each new technical advance generates new behaviours, new dependencies, and new fractures within human lived experience. These cracks produce emotional fallout—fatigue, uncertainty, anxiety—which are, in turn, harvested and folded back into the system as data, as value, as markets. This does not exist as a process resultant from a glitch within the capitalist system circuit; this is *functional* design, a *feature* of *immediate modernity*. The logic of technology-capitalism rewards anything that sustains the cycle, even if that which is being sustained is collective deterioration. If anxiety can be understood as the primary system output (as positioned in Chapters 3 and 4), then this is an acceptable social artefact, as this human anxiety, while exponentially rising, becoming ever more intolerable and unsustainable, itself becomes a site of investment. If disaffection, addiction, or malaise emerge, these constructs too are monetised in different ways that appear as if capital is presenting the solution. To clarify, capital processes are presenting a *pseudo* solution, but they are extending a solution to the primary problem that capital itself creates; thus, a self-perpetuating feedback circuit: *the structure consumes its own consequences as fuel and asks for more.* As this framework is embedded as structural hegemony, such process occurs largely invisible to social actors; they see their negative experiences less as a product of *immediate modernity* and simply as a naturalised *hyper-visible* framing of modern existence—of *evolving progress*. Accepting this position, we must now recognise that it is becoming increasingly negative to remain alive in *immediate modernity*, and natural anxiety, anomie and tensions associated with existence drive many to internalise this disquieted position: that existing in *immediate modernity* carries inherent negatives and these are inescapable human experiences while operating under contemporary capitalist sovereignty. While the system frames this affect as *illness*, it is likely that this affection will intensify as the system continues to upgrade itself. Via this analytic frame, acceleration no longer signals the possibility of rupture or release but the stable operating condition of *immediate modernity*. The system's very ability to absorb its own crises, repackage its failures as innovation, and transform decay into productivity illustrates the complete deterritorialisation of critique itself. The speed of collapse is reabsorbed as growth and the mechanics of breakdown reconstituted as proof of vitality. This diagnostic turn marks a crucial theoretical shift; it clarifies that acceleration represents less a tactic to be enacted, and constitutes instead a pathology to be studied: an epistemic artefact of a society that confuses movement with meaning. To read *The Decline* through i/Acc is therefore to map how such misrecognition becomes the defining logic of the present: the conversion of exhaustion into momentum, and of terminal collapse into continuous operation.

10.2 Embedded Pathologising of the Social

The most insidious aspect of this negative experience loop is how it renders collective breakdown as private malfunction. As outlined in Chapters 2, 3, and 4, experiences of anxiety, which emerge in tandem with disruptive societal and technological shifts, are now always individuated. Rather than anxious social consternations being recognised as symptoms of systemic dysfunction, they are packaged as personal defects for which capital has the answer. Treatments are rolled out that attempt to make individuals 'function' again: *in effect, to make them compatible with a system that is making them ill*. Standardised scales, chemical interventions, behaviourist therapies—all aim to bring the individual back to some *imagined baseline of normal*. But, this 'normal' is defined by the very system that is also accelerating *decline*. So, the subject is returned to 'functionality' but that functionality is measured against a broken metric, rendering true recovery within the system an impossibility as recovery would require an exit from the system itself.

10.3 Hyperstitional Logic and the Flatline-Inhabited Future

Linking with these positions: earlier I introduced hyperstition (Chapters 7 and 8), the concept that certain fictions, when believed, produce the conditions for their own realisation. This is key to understanding how *The Decline* has been rendered both imaginable, acceptable, and eventually ***naturalised*** as the hegemonic reality of ***immediate modernity***. We as human actors are constantly fed imagined visions of future-facing narratives that promise technological solutionism while simultaneously preparing us for collapse. The logic is: ***everything will get better, but only after it gets worse, and the worse is already here, so get used to it***. Through this dynamic, *The Decline* is no longer ***rendered*** to us as a potential, it takes on the form of a structural, programmed inevitability. Our timelines, expectations, and emotional landscapes begin to become shaped in ways that foreclose real alternatives, much like Fisher argues vis-à-vis capitalist realism (Fisher, 2022). We—social actors—exist in a future that has already been sold to us as pre-wrapped and padded with crisis management, market opportunities, and lifestyle tweaks. This drives the rationale that there is no escape from this invasive and pro-anxious culture, only the possibility to upgrade forward into an improved reality; however, the ***true reality*** is that this upgraded construct contains the same negatives as the past, now superseded, version of existence. While new solutions are offered, these are reactive to the issues that have been replicated into the new assembly, but (as per above), the onus of such problems are increasingly localised as the responsibilities—*the failings*—of the individual, ***not*** the system itself that manufactures and reanimates these glitches. Thus, 'progress' within ***immediate modernity*** can be conceptualised, as William S. Burroughs alluded to (Burroughs, 1982), as a virus; it replicates the most 'stable' portions of capital code based on the successes of the past programme logics to evolve this into a new 'improved' human-project, but, and reading Beck here (Beck, 2009, 2014) this evolved code carries with it the corruptions that dictated the necessity for evolution, which themselves evolve in magnitude and effects alongside the core base-code of the system. As such, the problems continue to follow and become increasingly indelibly influential with each replication cycle, and indeed—more naturalised as normality and progressively read as 'just the way that things are'. As this technology-capitalism loop tightens through increasingly frequent replications and updates, another emergent development gains ground: the progressive normalisation of digital interactions as not simply a part of human life, but synonymous—*naturally networked*—with existence in continually upgrading technoreality. This *hypernormalisation* of emotional interactions with *flatline constructs* signals a key turn in technological sensemaking, human-machine relations, and shaping human behaviour. We are being conditioned to seek emotional fulfilment, community, even transcendence, through increasingly elaborate and responsive virtual spaces and *flatlines*, that are becoming symbiotically more human-like due to their interactions with humans: driven by the data of human interactions, but in turn are also directly influencing human interactions through this normalised engagement. Where Fisher once asked whether *flatline constructs* are truly 'dead' (Fisher, 1999), the much more urgent question today is whether humans are now only deemed 'alive' in relation to their performance within technological systems and their increasing relationship of reliance upon these once so-called 'dead' machinic constructs.

This focus on *flatline* interactions co-occurs with shifting norms for how social connections are valued and desired in *immediate modernity*. What now matters in society is not *being*, but commodified activity: the production of affect, the appearance of engagement, the display of a symbolic avatar, and the outward production into the capitalist machine of curated performances evidencing *a life well lived* and how this was achieved. Considering the role of social media in *immediate modernity* and growing AI-integration with every aspect of society, *the flatline*, via this frame, no longer spotlights a division between human and non-human; it now represents a *field* upon which networked experiences are played out: a platform encapsulating a new anxious normal where emotions, memories, and presentations of *being* are reduced to commodification via organising measures of how 'liked' and 'shared' they are. Thus, human value has been abridged via interconnections with the machinic: the viewing of experience through the lens of the digital world and the virtual field. It is no longer machines mimicking human behaviour; humans adapt themselves to become more like functional *machinic* constructs: always online, always updating, always optimising and reading data, performing upgrades and developing new programmes, and sharing new information. A salient lens from which to frame this comparison is an extended position to the one I use to close Chapter 9: what happens to humans during downtime? If a construct idles without engagement like

Dixie Flatline in *Neuromancer* (Gibson, 1984), this mimics the devaluation of any human who is not economically or socially productive within the capitalist hegemony. In contrast, if *flatline constructs* continue to grow, learn, or create in downtime, they begin to surpass the limited expectations placed on most humans within capitalist frames. This inversion, the potential obsolescence of the human, is not far-fetched science fiction or a starting point for hyperstition; it is embedded in the tangible and evolving tendency to outsource emotional labour, creativity, memory, and desire to technological systems. It is more than simply humans evolving to live *through* our devices; it is now that these systems increasingly and symbiotically live through *us*; and as they do, the line between user and used, actor and acted upon becomes increasingly blurred.

10.4 Decline as the System 'Working Properly'

This 'working properly' argument is the uncomfortable core assertion of this summarising chapter: *The Decline* is not a misfire; it is the machine running smoothly. All the psychic, relational, and social turbulence we humans are currently living through is, perversely, the result of *immediate modernity* meeting its internal goals. Growth, extraction, speed, abstraction: these are not to be considered side effects of capitalism, they are capital's root circuitry. Even if the world collapses under the affective anxiety conjured by the present hegemonic control system, this is *not* a reason for the system to be triggered to reduce acceleration. Destruction is understood under this hegemony as an opportunity to innovate, disrupt, and monetise the fallout state. Thus, technocapitalism does not resist total thresholds, it actively chases them. Through this framing, collapse vectors fail to represent system interruptions, instead, they highlight a future deliverable. What the present accelerating, upgrading, and paradoxically self-consuming/preserving framework is chasing is **terminal destruction** of the human, and this is the natural, programmed and desirable endpoint of the present structural capital system.

10.5 i/Acc: Directions for Empirical and Conceptual Inquiry

Reactive to the above four positions, i/Acc emerges from the recognition that traditional accelerationist projects, whether intensifying capital's flows or amplifying emancipatory accelerations, have stalled under the conditions of *immediate modernity*. Technological hegemony absorbs critique, neutralises resistance, and converts attempted redirections into another circuit of system-preservation even while that system points towards terminal destruction. Within this landscape, acceleration is a symptom as opposed to a strategy; a sign of a system optimising its own exhaustion. i/Acc reframes accelerationism as a diagnostic method rather than a prescriptive political programme. Its task is not to accelerate, stall, or 'disrupt' for emancipation, nor to seek a new revolutionary horizon, but to expose how capital's recursive loops function, where agency collapses, and how desires, behaviours, and infrastructures are captured, modulated, and reproduced. i/Acc proceeds from the assertion that *everyone is now an accelerationist*, less through ideology, but via structural complicity: each interaction, resistance, compliance, and pause, feeds the same intensifying machine. As such, the question is how to think and intervene within this condition without reproducing intrinsic and governing hegemonic trajectories. i/Acc responds by treating flows, glitches, stagnations and repetitions as empirical data: evidence of how acceleration operates as capital's stabilising logic rather than its destabilising force. It uses the speed of the system as a lens, a way of tracking its self-protective behaviours and identifying the boundaries of possible action. Where earlier /Acc threads either surrendered to capital's velocity (Land and E/Acc) or sought to weaponise/operationalise selective accelerations for egalitarian ends (L/Acc threads), i/Acc offers what these frameworks muted: a systematic method for *seeing* the system first, its constraints, circuits, and self-regulating mechanisms, before proposing any modulations. It does not seek purity, rupture or escape; it prioritises clarity, exposure, and practical re-routing within a reality where the system has already won. i/Acc invites translation into interdisciplinary, empirical inquiry; the i/Acc framework can be used to trace how individuals, institutions, and digital infrastructures internalise and reproduce accelerations that exhaust them, whether through algorithmic economies, attention architectures, automated labour, or affective infrastructures that convert anxiety into engagement. As both theory and method, i/Acc provides a toolkit (Chapter 6) for mapping the lived textures of systemic acceleration, textures that exist as evidence of a civilisation optimising its own *decline*.

10.6 Summary

In the context summarised by the above five points (and outlined via the combined chapters of this work), this book names the field of ***decline studies*** as a means to network the threads of anxiety, hyperstition, technocapital hegemony, contemporary *flatline* dynamics, and i/Acc into a coherent diagnostic frame, offering a contribution that should reignite interest in mapping our present *immediate* state, and illuminating a pathway for analytically thinking through *The Decline* rather than being paralysed by this reality. This is how this collective work should be read: a catalyst towards a radical embracing of the anxieties, tensions, and complications of the present moment, and a call for a progressively interpretative diagnostic approach to what can be done to move to a position of understanding, and then informed action.

References

Beck, U. (2009). *World at risk*. Polity.

Beck, U. (2014). *Ulrich Beck: Pioneer in cosmopolitan sociology and risk society*. Springer.

Burroughs, W. S. (1982). *Ah Pook is here and other texts*. Riverrun Press.

Fisher, M. (1999). *Flatline constructs: Gothic materialism and cybernetic theory-fiction* (Doctoral dissertation). University of Warwick.

Fisher, M. (2022). *Capitalist realism: Is there no alternative?* John Hunt Publishing.

Gibson, W. (1984). *Neuromancer*. Harper Voyager.

Postscript

Thomas: It will get better. Everything will be alright…
Anders: Except it won't you know.
Oslo, August 31st (2011, directed by Joachim Trier)
Nothing human makes it out of the near-future.
Nick Land (1994, Meltdown. See Land, 1995)

Ok, so what now? Is there a life after the loop? If *The Decline* is where we are located within *immediate modernity*, and the circuit is closed, is there anything left outside of this hegemony from which to assemble an escape trajectory and is such a mission possible? Reflecting honestly on the content of this work and the previous ten chapters, this is not the place for optimistic detours or techno-saviour fantasies to be constructed. However, perhaps there is space for a kind of refusal to be articulated, a refusal to continue pretending that everything is fine, or forever natural, or inevitable. Naming *The Decline* for what it is: an *immediate* destination, is a small act of resistance. Perhaps the language and structuring in this work will allow us to reimagine what might exist beyond repeated failed upgrades and static technological fragmentation, and strive for something better, more meaningful, and intrinsically *true and authentic* than simply optimisation and feeding core capital system functionality. Considering this position, we may not be able to step cleanly outside the loop. But, identifying the loop, mapping it, and pointing to its paradoxical rational absurdity, this is how we begin our journey towards a final

N. N. Adams, *Terminal Destruction*,
https://doi.org/10.1007/978-3-032-22274-9

escape, and this is the core function of this collective work. To aid this, I return primarily to the i/Acc theorising from Chapter 6 and leave you with the following overall summary in terms of forward progress:

Firstly, (and speaking most to the content of Chapters 5, 6 and 9) the most persistent thread in contemporary /Acc debate regarding the 'repurposing' of capital has centred on the stagnation of Left Accelerationist theory. Many argue that meaningful progress requires clarity around which capital-linked structures ought to be accelerated/decelerated/repurposed and in what ways, to re-circuit these frameworks and forge a pathway towards egalitarian futures. Yet, as this work has shown, such debates are increasingly entangled in the opacity of *immediate modernity*, particularly under the diffuse and ever-adaptive control of technological/technocapital hegemony. Via this lens, resistance is often neutralised through strategic obfuscation, while capital and its auxiliary systems are continuously amplified as a by-product of this resistance: capital does not collapse under resistance/intensification, it only absorbs this fuel and continues to adapt and grow. This must be accepted as the current de facto conceptualisation of the capital machine. Reconfiguring the machine to a point of (selective) collapse/reorientation without sufficient investigatory groundwork is double-edged and untenable due to the psychic and social damage, the potential *friendly fire* that such an 'overload' position conjures through supporting the machine itself[1].

To progress, L/Acc needs reinvigoration through renewed theoretical effort. Despite this, there is widespread recognition that L/Acc itself has stalled. This work addresses this impasse by offering a clarified account of L/Acc, distinguishing it from emerging strands, reconstructing foundational accelerationist texts, and proposing new frameworks through which the tradition might evolve, namely i/Acc. Building on the analysis of capital hegemony developed through each of this work's chapters, I argue that in a practical and systemic sense, we are now all accelerationists, and technocapital hegemony and our complicit support of this must be recognised. Whether through complicity, coercion, or attempted

[1] This paradox emerges when the logics of capital force resistance to be mobilised through capitalist mechanisms, converting anti-capitalist politics into commodities. As a simple example, protest T-shirts, produced through global supply chains and marketed via social media, circulate dissent within capitalism itself, transforming resistance into a harmless, consumable identity rather than a mobilising material challenge to capitalist hegemony.

resistance, contemporary life is saturated by mechanisms that intensify and sustain capital's functional reach. This totalising landscape demands a strategic response, and if L/Acc-linked positions are to move forward, we must first reckon with the networked complexity of *immediate modernity*: the specific contours of technological hegemony, *flatline constructs*, hyperstition, and the ways in which structures of constraint and domination operate under restrictive, self-perpetuating logics. Only then can we make informed judgements about which elements of capital and social infrastructure *should* be retooled, intensified, or dismantled and indeed which *can be*. While it may seem obvious which systems to empower and which to suppress, this work spotlights such clarity to be illusory. Even ostensibly progressive *left* accelerations carry unseen risks and unintended consequences. Considering this, I propose (in Chapter 6) the formalisation of a new theoretical paradigm: Investigative Accelerationism. This framework builds upon the groundwork laid here, aiming to re-open L/Acc discourse, assert its relevance within critical theory, and rigorously examine its foundational assumptions. i/Acc is explicitly concerned with interrogating technological hegemony and identifying which elements of capital can be both strategically accelerated and/or strategically decelerated in service of L/Acc's core aims: social equity, collective wellbeing, and a just future that fractures the present capital loop of *immediate modernity*. This theorising also advocates for new, reflective engagements with L/Acc's limitations: its internal contradictions, blind spots, and embedded risks. i/Acc is forward-looking and collaborative by design; it invites transdisciplinary work both within and beyond the academy and insists on ongoing critical engagement with emerging forms of accelerationism, including those aligned with L/Acc goals, such as Xenofeminism. I argue that this progress is assembled under the label of *Decline Studies*. The goal is to craft a dynamic, responsive theoretical practice, one that continually tests its assumptions against the reality of intensifying capital logics, and that remains attuned to both the promise and peril of acceleration. Please take what has been developed here and continue to grow this approach in any way you see fit that aligns with the above points.

Secondly, in practically confronting 'head-on' *The Decline* and its closed-loop structure, a form of accepted identity-renegotiation as rational ego death emerges as a necessary functional response to withdrawing from reliance upon the structuring framework that forms capital hegemony: a deliberate unmaking of the self as it is bound within the accelerating circuits of *immediate modernity*. This process of ego dissolution conforms to a form of resistance and adaptation, enabling a rupture from the internalised logics of technological hegemony and capital saturation. To translate this towards operationalisation: we as social actors *must* learn to *care less* about the tacit control of capital hegemony as networked within our lives and all facets of this: buy less, avoid advertising; resist digital depictions of the self, continual technological upgrading and integrations; normalise prolonging the inevitable obsolescence of technological artefacts instead of accepting this—hack, stitch together, break-open, repurpose and prioritise these hallmarks as central facets of *our resisting selves*. Situated within the framework of i/Acc, ego death (identity negotiations and reconfigurations to decentralise capital processes as a marker of self-identity) can be understood as a vital gesture that exposes and destabilises the entanglements of identity, agency, and control that sustain, naturalise and embed the capital loop. This actively challenges the illusion of autonomous subjectivity, recognising instead the systemic forces that shape and limit possibility: it *resists* complicit consent to existence within this hegemony. By embracing this 'rational ego death', we open space for reimagining modes of collective existence that evade or subvert the imperative of capital optimisation, upgrading and expansion, carving out openings for alternative temporalities and relationalities. This personal internalisation of the i/Acc ethos reflects i/Acc's broader ambition to move beyond stagnation by spotlighting which structures require acceleration, deceleration, or radical transformation, and recognising that such shifts begin with an inward reckoning that dissolves the boundaries imposed by the machinery of *The Decline*. Ego death thus becomes a strategy to cope with *immediate modernity*, a site where personal and political transformation intersect, enabling us to reconfigure the loop, as a first step, from within, and imagine futures beyond the system's relentless reproduction: we can dream our own futures, conjure these into hyperstitional being, in actualities that resist and overwrite the programmed narrative that is force-fed to us. This, at least, is something of a start point for functional resistance.

As I said in the foreword: good luck. The future is ours, but only if we refuse the one already sold to us and allow ourselves to imagine alternatives.

Reference

Land, N. (1995). *Meltdown*. In *N. Land, Fanged Noumena: Collected Writings 1987–2007* (pp. 441–460). Urbanomic.

N. N. Adams, *Terminal Destruction*,
https://doi.org/10.1007/978-3-032-22274-9

Index

N. N. Adams, *Terminal Destruction*,
https://doi.org/10.1007/978-3-032-22274-9

The manufacturer's authorised representative in the EU is Springer Nature Customer Service Centre GmbH, Europaplatz 3, 69115 Heidelberg, Germany. If you have any concerns regarding our products, please contact ProductSafety@springernature.com

Printed and bound by CPI Group (UK) Ltd, Croydon, CR0 4YY
21/09/2026
02219963-0001